Feels Like Far

BOOKS BY LINDA HASSELSTROM

Bitter Creek Junction
Feels Like Far: A Rancher's Life on the Great Plains
Bison: Monarch of the Plains (nonfiction)
The Roadside History of South Dakota
Dakota Bones: Collected Poems
Land Circle: Writings Collected from the Land
Going Over East: Reflections of a Woman Rancher
Windbreak: A Woman Rancher on the Northern Plains
Roadkill
Caught by One Wing

BOOKS EDITED BY LINDA HASSELSTROM

Woven on the Wind: Women Write About Friendship in the Sagebrush West
(with Gaydell Collier and Nancy Curtis)

Leaning into the Wind: Women Write from the Heart of the West
(with Gaydell Collier and Nancy Curtis)

Journal of a Mountain Man by James Clyman

Feels Like Far

A Rancher's Life on the Great Plains

Linda Hasselstrom

A Mariner Book

Houghton Mifflin Company

Boston   New York

First Mariner Books edition 2001

Copyright © 1999 by Linda Hasselstrom
Reprinted by arrangement with The Lyons Press

For information about permission to reproduce selections from this book, write to Permissions, Houghton Mifflin Company, 215 Park Avenue South, New York, New York 10003.

Visit our Web site: www.houghtonmifflinbooks.com.

Library of Congress Cataloging-in-Publication Data is available.

ISBN 0-618-12495-0 (pbk.)

Printed in the United States of America

QUM 10 9 8 7 6 5 4 3 2 1

Contents

Prologue: The Hawk Hits the Window   *1*

The Owl in the Dark   *11*

Sonata for Horses   *21*

Blues for Shoveling Horse Manure   *33*

Reckoning the Cost of a Dead Steer   *45*

Lightning Strikes the White Heifer   *57*

Looking for the Dark: Buffalo Winter   *71*

Beekeeper   *87*

Badger's Business   *107*

Looking for Death: The Deer Harvest   *119*

The Young Cow: Going Back to Grass   *139*

Looking for the Light: The Elk in the Aspen   *153*

Climbing into the Bull Pen   *167*

Nighthawks Fly in Thunderstorms   *185*

Looking for Life: Fire in the Wildlife Pasture   *199*

Badger's Daughter   *211*

Epilogue: Spinning with the Hawks   *221*

Acknowledgments   *231*

Prologue:
The Hawk Hits
the Window

Looking back at the first fifty years of my life is a bit like flying over the great high plains prairie stretching from the Missouri River on the east to the Rocky Mountains on the west, from the southern tip of Texas to the Canadian border. All I can see from the height of an airplane is an outline of reality. Looking carefully, I might see a ranch yard with its attached corrals and water tanks, perhaps a house surrounded by a green lawn contrasting with the tawny native grasses reaching into the distance. My eyes might trace cattle trails from nearby hills converging on a spot of green where a glint of sunlight on water marks a water tank.

Still, from the height of an airplane or a half century of life, I see only isolated vignettes, not the details of the landscape. From this height, I might miss the coyote concealed under sagebrush, sniffing the wind before he begins to hunt moles in the grass. Looking in one direction, I could overlook the skunk deftly avoiding the first cow coming for a drink. To inhale the skunk's sharp fear mingled in the breeze with a sagebrush tang, I'd need to be on the ground, dusty and sunburned.

So I tell stories of my grasslands home as I might fly over my past, relating information significant to me, incidents I now believe were important in shaping my beliefs. A different narrator would see different events.

"How long does it take to write a good book?" asked Edward Abbey in A Voice Crying in the Wilderness, *answering himself, "All of the years that you've lived." As I look at my past for clues to my future, I wonder—can I write about the ranch and the prairie now that I live in a city? What will the changes in my life mean to me as a woman? As a rancher? As a writer?*

For one whose senses and emotions are alive home is anywhere.

—EDWARD ABBEY

My connections to the grasslands of western South Dakota may have begun long before my birth, with ancestors who settled on the broad western plain in Dakota Territory and in the rumpled valleys of the nearby Black Hills. But I was born in Texas, and I didn't see the prairie ranch around which the rest of my life has revolved until I was nine years old. Almost at once I began writing down what I saw and thought, linking the ranch with the act of writing. As an adult, I have come to believe that both my physical life and my spirit are so deeply connected to that particular plot of land, the family ranch, that I might be a stalk of grass myself, rooted in arid and meager soil.

Somewhere I've read that the Navajo people often bury a daughter's umbilical cord under the floor where the loom stands, to attract her toward the weaving of blankets, her future occupation and art. A boy's umbilical is usually buried in the sheep corral to focus his attention entirely on the well-being of the flock: make him "sheep-minded." The souls of the living may wander at night around the place where the umbilical cord is buried. My ancestors performed their religious rites in a specific building on a special day, but a Navajo may conduct her spiritual ceremonies privately, in a certain site in a particular landscape. As soon as I learned of this Navajo manner of prayer, I identified with it.

For nearly forty years I lived on the ranch land my father's father homesteaded in 1899. I grew up absorbed in the arid landscape and its people. I dutifully went to college, got married to a divorced man with three children, and when he decided to live elsewhere, I went along. But when the marriage fell apart, I returned to the ranch. All the elements that became part of my life when I first moved there—neighbors, cows, relatives, deer, weather, water, clods of dirt, and the connections between them—grew naturally into my writing.

At thirty-five, I was happy in my work and my life. With my second husband, George, I built a house on a hill above my parents' buildings and settled down to ranch and write, beginning to believe we really could live as the fairy tales of my childhood promised, happily ever after. With a deep sense of recognition, I adopted another Navajo custom. Preparing to pray, a Navajo woman picks specific plants or makes an offering at the stream where she draws water, in order to remind the holy people of that particular place that she belongs there. Her ritualized actions establish communication with the spiritual element of that spot, and each time the woman returns, she can be confident that its people, its spirits, will know her, welcome and comfort her. If she should move to a new land—rare among her people—she will have to get acquainted with the spirits of that new land, settle herself among them by learning their names and where they may be found. This connection between the land and the spiritual life of the people who dwell there seemed so clearly logical that I accepted it at once. Living on the ranch, I had always known where I was, felt my place in my flesh and guts. Planting trees for a windbreak north of our new ranch house, seeding wildflowers, I confirmed and deepened my bonds to the land.

Then, when I was forty-five years old, my husband, George R. Snell, died of a malignant tumor caused by the radiation doctors used to treat the Hodgkin's disease he'd battled for years. The news that his condition was terminal came only a few days before his death. During that traumatic time, both George and I were comforted by the presence of our friend Jerry. Once, when he and George were trapping together in the winter in a remote Wyoming location, the tipi caught fire in the middle of the night. George pulled Jerry from the flames, raced him to a hospital eighty miles away, and cared for him while his severely burned hands healed. Jerry, who had settled into a job with the Wyoming Department of Transportation in Cheyenne, returned the favor by staying with us in the hospital until George died and helping me arrange the funeral.

Unable to sleep much during that first long winter after George died, I did as I'd been trained to do from childhood: I worked. I kept helping my father, feeding cows and plodding ahead with my writing while I settled George's estate and examined my prospects. I stained the cupboard doors George left unfinished and built bookshelves to line the basement. George and I were in that house no less than it was in us, and I expected to remain there for the rest of my life.

———

I realized I'd made a mistake a few months into my seven-year marriage to my first husband, Daniel. He was as reliable as plains weather: you couldn't be sure about either one moment to the next. My second husband, George, was a model of loyalty for ten years, but the dead don't offer much practical help with life's daily dilemmas.

My father was part of my life longer than either husband, and his beliefs and discipline formed the foundations of my character. But as his mind and body began to crumble, I found it progressively more difficult to work with him. After George died, my father began treating me like a child. One spring, several cows died in a single day during calving season. By nightfall, the barn was full of orphan calves. Over the next few days we struggled to understand and stop the deaths, feed the hungry calves, and tend the rest of the herd while my father talked incessantly about the cow that died first. "You're too young to understand," he said, "because it's never happened to you. You don't know how it feels to have something just drop, just be dead beside you. Alive one minute, dead the next."

Finally, my body worn out and my patience gone, I yelled back, "I watched my husband die! I'm pretty well acquainted with it, thank you!"

My father looked at me, his face cunning. "You've got to grow up," he said, "and get over that habit of exaggerating everything."

Then one day my father gave me an ultimatum: to stop writing and work as his hired hand for $300 a month, or to leave the ranch and never come back. That same day, I loaded my dog, Frodo, and a few possessions into my car and fled three hundred miles southwest to take refuge with Jerry in Cheyenne, Wyoming's capital city.

I felt like a fugitive from my family, from my home, from my experiences as a rancher, and from the future I had planned. My mind circled back to my childhood as I tried to understand what had happened to my father and how to help him. It crossed my mind that I might have to choose either to give up the ranch or to fight him for control of it.

Arriving in Cheyenne, I had no particular strategy. I was taking refuge in my long friendship with Jerry, confident his calm and strength would help me figure out what to do next. We had been friends for more than twenty years. Then, two years after George died, we spent three weeks traveling in Scotland together and became lovers. After the trip, we'd considered living together, but, with my father's behavior already deteriorating, I decided to remain on the ranch, while Jerry stayed in Cheyenne because of his career.

After my father's outburst, I packed up and moved to Wyoming where Jerry and I found a house together in Cheyenne. I returned to my ranch house a few days later to find my father pleasant and puzzled about my move. I began going back to the ranch almost every week to help him with work he couldn't do alone, but each time I left, I took a few more of my possessions. Beginning my new life with Jerry, ten years my junior, I was in conflict with myself. I spent most of my time pondering the past, unconsciously searching for a way to return to the life I knew.

———

The sagebrush plains around Cheyenne are similar to those around the ranch, but I woke to a strange world every morning. The horizon outside my window was filled with buildings instead of sky and grass. Every day, I brooded over my father's behavior, hoping to find a way to keep him from destroying his life's work and himself, wondering if I was too old and persnickety to learn new habits.

Outside the bedroom window, one quarter mile upwind, stood an oil refinery. Atop a tall smokestack, fires incinerated excess vapor day and night, flavoring every breath with crude oil. "Live like your hair is on fire," says a Buddhist maxim. As theory, the saying is attractive: live each moment fully, as though you may die tomorrow. George believed it, and so do I. But those flames reflected in the mirrors on the closet doors gave me nightmares of being cremated alive.

Next door lived a trucker who worked at night. During the day, he mowed his lawn and repaired engines. From the open windows of the house across the street poured rap music played at full volume night and day, along with the guttural and profane shouts of the three young men who lived there. Beside them lived a man with a pickup truck sporting a bumper sticker proclaiming it saved by Jesus. The engine told a different story. On weekends, he ran the motor at full throttle while he peered under its hood, no doubt praying for its soul. In the small yards behind many of the houses in the neighborhood were penned large dogs. Every time one of them protested its confinement, every other dog within miles barked. After trying for days to ignore all this racket, I concluded that the most annoying sounds in the symphony were produced by little dogs that squealed incessantly without apparently stopping for breath.

City noises kept me unsettled, but they were only part of my bewilderment. I had learned to walk with sure steps on the prairie around the ranch even in darkness, my path lit only by moonlight, because I knew the countryside so intimately. I settled into that place so thoroughly that the land and its inhabitants knew me, by sight, by scent, by carriage, by light, and by darkness.

To go somewhere in this city, I studied directions as if preparing for a quiz, and still I often failed. "Meet me at the Chinese restaurant for lunch at twelve," Jerry might say, and I would gaily agree. Cannily, I kept a map of the city in my car. I would leave fifteen minutes early and recite the turns as I drove. By the appointed hour, I usually knew approximately where I was and how to get where I should have been, but I was rarely in the right spot.

Suddenly I had been transformed from a mature woman of wisdom into a moron. I blushed when Jerry's long-suffering friends repeated directions. Even the patient ones must have wondered why getting around the city was so hard for me. My memory wasn't faulty—as a teacher, I prided myself on knowing my students' names on the third day of class. The problem lay deeper.

On my horse in South Dakota, out of sight of the Black Hills marking the western horizon, I could feel their blue weight looming and knew in which direction the gates lay. Take me to any spot on or near our land, spin me around until I grew dizzy, and, like a compass, I would point toward home. Determined to learn how to navigate in the city, I spent days going to garage sales. I wandered blithely off, assuming I would be lost and determined to enjoy the experience and learn from it. Gradually, I began to find locations more easily. And I understood my confusion.

Like many cities, Cheyenne was laid out in a grid, which allowed for the growth its founders predicted. Here, streets are aligned with the railroad tracks; transportation companies provided freight and passenger services fundamental to the city's growth. On a map, the square of that original plan is clearly visible, but those early planners used crude instruments. Outside the cube, later surveyors aligned streets to true north, so streets running through the square make sudden turns. On the ranch, the Black Hills stand on the western horizon, so I had a ready reference; in Cheyenne, no mountains nail down my personal compass, though the gold gleam of the capitol dome sometimes gives me a clue.

Finally, I realized that I didn't navigate by the symbols most people use. I was not in the habit of looking at street signs. Instead, I noticed natural landmarks. To reach the post office, I turned right at a patch of flax and blue fescue. The library was straight ahead when I saw the sidewalk lined with sagebrush, across from the witch's house surrounded by unruly coneflowers, Shasta daisies, and blanketflowers.

I walked Frodo every day in a city park where I once saw a hawk cruising over the shallow lake. I shaded my eyes and squinted: yes, a redtail. Then the hawk swung into a fast arc. Deceived by the reflection of sky in an uncurtained window in a nearby apartment complex, the hawk crashed into the glass. I heard the smack of the collision and saw the hawk drop into a cluster of junipers, then recover and soar away. I knew the hawk, but I couldn't name any of the streets around the park. In trying to learn my way around Cheyenne, I was placing new information on top of a map of my native habitat, a map carved into my flesh and bones, a pattern so deeply buried in my brain as to be nearly instinctual.

At first, the only way I could decode directions in the city was by visualizing the center of my personal universe, my ranch home. I pictured myself standing on that hill in South Dakota, beside the home I now call Windbreak House. With north at my back, east lies on my left hand. Of course, I know where the sun rises in Cheyenne, so I could point my left hand to the east and find north.

This disorientation, more profound than being lost, gave me a sensation of drifting, of levitation. I was without an anchor after four decades of knowing my location in every drop of my blood. I got dizzy walking down the street. In daylight, seeing the red and yellow blooms of blanketflowers sometimes calmed me enough to figure out where I belonged for the moment.

While I considered where I belong in a larger sense, I created a miniature prairie around our city house. In beds along the street I placed prairie iris from my South Dakota hillside. I tucked a cutting from my grandmother's peony beside the front gate to wait for another spring. After we gave away the swing set in the backyard and shoveled the gravel into the alley, I dug a garden plot by hand

and planted corn, basil, and tomatoes. Digging in the soil reminded me how consistent the earth is, despite the frantic and constant clamor of the people who live on its skin. Gardening exercises my body and sustains my brain. Sprinkling my aunt's hollyhock seed along the back fence one day, I noticed a currant bush like the one by my mother's back door. During cold winter days, I mused, I would see the bare bush each time I put the garbage in the alley. No matter how gray the city seemed, I could anticipate April, when the currant bush would be covered in yellow blooms shaped like trumpets. I sank into a memory of sitting on my parents' back steps as a child, inhaling its spicy odor, pulling off a blossom to taste the drop of honey at its tip.

I could not stop writing, even though I had been dropped into a web of city streets. Day after day, while my mind spun in confusion, I kept scribbling entries in the journal of my existence, learning new ways home through the maze.

Mari Sandoz, who grew up in the Nebraska Sandhills not far from my ranch home, was one of my early heroines as a woman and a writer. She, too, worked so hard on the family's homestead as a child that she carried the scars to the grave, and her father, like mine, called writers and artists the "maggots of society."

Sandoz eventually moved to New York, continuing to write with power about her own landscape. When city readers didn't believe her tales of life on the plains, she defended the truth she knew: "My nonfiction is really nonfiction. This side of the Hudson there is a difference." Sandoz's stories—both those she wrote and those she lived—have inspired me since I first began writing at the age of nine. Her words reflect the country I know more deeply than I know any human. If she kept writing, even in New York, perhaps I can learn to make a new song in my Wyoming exile.

The Owl
in the Dark

*Looking at my mother's photo album during a night when city noises
keep me from sleeping, I realize again how ignorant I am of her life
before she became my mother. In her favorite high school picture, she
stands with one arm raised behind her head, back straight so her breasts
stick out. Thin shoulder straps support a gauzy dress ending at mid-thigh.
Her mouth is outlined in dark lipstick and is pursed into an exaggerated
pout. Posed like a film star, she is beautiful enough to be one, a fantasy I
never shared. She once told me that since I couldn't rely on my looks to
get me security in the form of a husband, I'd better get an education. As a
teenager, I usually wore torn jeans and western shirts a boy cousin had
outgrown. Only now can I begin to sympathize with Mother's frustration
when, as soon as I could walk, I headed outdoors to get dirty.*

*The photos in her album don't always match Mother's stories.
Several pictures show her staring deadpan at the camera from a street
lined with towering buildings, holding a lipstick-stained cigarette and
wearing a broad hat tilted over her upswept hair. Several other photos
show her with a cocktail glass, yet she taught me that ladies don't smoke
or drink. I know she went to secretarial school in a small Nebraska town
where even today none of the buildings is more than three stories high.
When was she smoking cigarettes and drinking martinis in a city? I asked*

once. *"I married my high school sweetheart and moved to Pittsburgh,"* she said without looking at me. *"I shouldn't have done it, because I never loved him."* She divorced her first husband to marry my father, Paul, a short man with dark eyes under a tilted hat brim, who appeared in her album a few pages later. Other pictures show him in dashing poses—riding a motorcycle or standing beside his plane. Though he was my biological father, I've never seen any physical resemblance between us. Only when I have followed an impulse to quit a job in anger, or throw a flowerpot at a wandering husband, have I heard Paul chuckling inside my skull.

When I was a few days old, he took a picture of Mother with me. *"He just wanted a baby so he wouldn't have to go in the army,"* she once explained. Mother, wearing a stylish dress, holds me at arm's length on her knee in the picture. A nanny hovers behind the screen door. My fat arms stick out of a pink lace gown. Mother wanted a daughter who would be a lady swathed in silk, but I was born to love denim. I see in that picture the distance between us, a chasm we can never cross.

As soon as we moved to the ranch, I aspired to become a cowgirl. If she buttoned me into a dainty outfit and sent me outside to wait while she dressed for church, I wrecked my clothes in seconds, no matter how hard I tried to stay clean. Mother would come out the door, perfectly garbed and smiling. Seconds later she would be screaming and slapping at me as she chased me into the house to change clothes.

But silence is where the victims dwell.

—Nelly Sachs
O the Chimneys

Pain nips at my neck and shoulder muscles, and words on the computer screen blur. I've been working for three hours without a break. I stretch and turn toward the bookshelves, hunting for my mother's worn copy of an Ogden Nash collection with a poem, "Adventures of Isabel," guaranteed to hurl me back to the evening I first heard it from my mother.

She came to tuck me in earlier than usual that night, and caught me poised at the bedroom door, bouncing on the balls of my feet. Then I flicked the bedroom light off and leapt to my bed on the other side of the room. When Mother saw me in midleap, she understood at once that I was trying to evade the creatures. She turned the light back on and knelt beside the bed, pulling me down beside her as she raised the bedspread to look underneath. "See," she said. "No monsters. Just dust bunnies." I knew the dust was proof that evil oozed through the floorboards in darkness. She thought it suggested I clean my room.

I slid under the covers, and she sat at the end of the bed to read to me about Isabel, a girl of few words and fast action. The poetic child immediately became my ideal, though I suspected that her parents insisted she wash her hands and comb her hair before combat. When she met a bear, she ate it. She turned a threatening witch into milk and drank her. She whacked off a giant's head and cured a doctor who tried to give her pills. If I ever consult a psychoanalyst—I'd have to be forced, at gunpoint and in handcuffs—my asocial behavior would probably be blamed on Ogden Nash. I was so enthusiastic about Isabel that I memorized the poem. When company came, Mother often made me stand up and recite it, insisting that a public performance would cure my shyness.

By the time my mother discovered that particular fear, we had escaped from Paul and were living in Rapid City, South Dakota, where Mother photographed me in a snowbank during the blizzard of 1949. I remember only disconnected scenes before then. In one, I am sitting on Mother's lap, trying to forget crouching under the kitchen table while she had screamed and smashed liquor bottles in the sink. I had watched my father's legs as he paced back and forth in the small kitchen, swearing and kicking shards of broken glass. I am afraid to remember my father's warm arms and the smell of his cigarettes and bourbon. If I cry, Mother will slap me again.

Instead, I look out the black window beside me, hoping she'll loosen her grip around me so my ribs will stop hurting. I listen to the train wheels rumble on the tracks, hearing a rhythm like the sound of horses' hooves in a radio program. The railway cars look as if they are uncoiling from a black pool, a snake wearing a chain of gold windows. Mother whispers over and over, "The sins of the fathers shall be visited on the children. Remember, darling, you must never drink liquor."

I know now that my mother ran away from my father because she caught him in bed with her best friend, that I was three years old when she carried me onto a passenger train in Galveston, Texas, that in Rapid City, she found work as a secretary to a law firm with offices in a bank. She persuaded her mother, my grandmother Cora, to leave her ranch in the southern Black Hills to care for me at first. Every day Grandmother plaited my hair into neat braids and held my hand as she walked with me to kindergarten. I remember having chicken pox only because I can see Grandmother sitting by my bed, spooning chicken soup between my dry lips.

When I was old enough to walk to kindergarten and back alone, Grandmother went back to her ranch. Every morning, Mother cautioned me not to light the stove or talk to strangers when I got home, but all I wanted to do was read or make up stories with my dolls. On winter evenings after the street grew dark and the other children had gone inside, I'd sometimes hide in the bushes at the end of our block until I heard her heels tapping on the sidewalk. Once I stepped out and said, "Boo!" When she screamed, a couple of neighborhood men burst out of their front doors, still carrying their napkins, running to her rescue. After that, I'd sing the refrain from *Cinderella* when I heard her coming. Some nights, she'd answer me from halfway down the block—"Bibbetty, bobbetty, boo." Usually she said, "I'm too tired to play. Come on out."

After supper, she washed dishes or studied her bills at the kitchen table while I undressed for bed. When I called, she'd come to read me a story if she wasn't too tired, then tuck me in and kiss me goodnight. After the night she read about Isabel, she often chose bedtime stories that emphasized bravery.

One day I came home to find Mother pouring coffee for a thin, tanned man sitting in our kitchen, a straw hat on his knee. John Hasselstrom's cheeks were brown, but his forehead was so white I saw blue veins pulsing above his eyes. Straight black hair fell over his high forehead. He smiled at me. Reaching into his pocket, he opened his hand, holding out a dime and a nickel.

"You can have either one," he said. "But not both." Leaning forward to look, I put my hands on his knees and was startled to feel the bones. I took the dime.

"Why did you take that one? It's smaller."

"It's worth more."

He beamed and patted my head. "You're a smart little girl."

I don't know how long my mother dated John, but I remember her thinking aloud that marriage to him would be a wise investment in her future and mine. She asked a friend in the bank to look up his accounts and came home singing that day. I whispered in my favorite teacher's ear, "My mother's getting married, and I'm going to have a horse and a daddy." I'd hardly known Paul, so I didn't expect a new father to change my life much. But a horse—I'd dreamed of horses as long as I could remember.

On Memorial Day weekend in 1952, my mother and John were married in Cheyenne, Wyoming, while I stayed with an aunt and uncle. On July 14, I celebrated my ninth birthday on the ranch. Exactly a month later, on August 14, we all drove to the county seat of Custer and met with a judge in long black robes. He made my father and mother wait on a hard wooden bench outside his door while he explained adoption to me. John would become my legal father, changing my name from Bovard to Hasselstrom, even on my birth certificate. He asked me if I wanted to be adopted, but I was so shy I probably only nodded. For a long time I carried in my diary a slip of paper with the judge's telephone number because he told me to call him if my father ever hurt me. I can see the man's craggy face still, feel the warmth of his promise. That day, when my name was changed to match my father's, my real life began.

In my first photo album is a picture of me with my mother before the old brick courthouse in Custer. Mother wears a white hat, gloves, and high heels. I'm wearing a ruffled plaid pinafore a little short for my bony legs. The toes of my white shoes are perfectly even. The strap of a new white purse crosses my shoulder and my left hand tightly grips the purse's snap top. I'm smiling—happy and scared and trying to keep my huge front teeth covered for the picture my father took to commemorate the day we became a family. Afterward, we ate dinner at an old log hotel in Custer State Park and had ice cream for dessert. In the gift shop, John bought me a Black Hills gold ring. Every year afterward until nearly the end of my father's life, my family quietly celebrated my "second birthday" on August 14.

For me, ranch life was like slipping my foot into a perfectly fitting soft boot smelling of oil and good leather. I had longed for prairie spaces before I had the least idea what distance was. Living in the country was coming home from a journey I already perceived as long.

My mother grew up in the same region, on her family's ranch in the southern Black Hills, anxious to escape. She hated getting her hands dirty and loved talking about city life. Settled at the ranch, she demanded and got a new house, new furniture and carpeting. My father refused to buy her a set of china, so a Ladies Aid group chipped in and bought it as a welcoming gift. For a while, she plunged into community life, singing in the choir and joining a church sewing and social group, but she quit both groups when they didn't do things her way. She fought ferociously with my father to keep me inside the house learning to clean and cook. She never gave up on trying to civilize me. While I grew to love the land and the cattle we raised, she saw the community and its residents as coarse and ignorant, the animals as a mass of witless creatures valuable only to provide grocery money and enough extra for new carpet every few years.

Still, at first she worked at being a perfect ranch wife. She created sumptuous lunches to take to my father in the hay field. When he came in dirty and tired, she'd say, "I made a picnic supper. Let's drive into the Hills."

"Wife," he'd reply, "I can't quit early in the middle of a hay crop." —

Once or twice she made reservations for dinner at Mount Rushmore and bought tickets for a theater production afterward. Each time, my father got back to the house late, filthy from pulling a calf or fixing a greasy piece of machinery. Mother would say, "Hurry and clean up. I laid your clothes out on the bed."

"No," he'd reply, standing in the kitchen with his hands on his hips. "I didn't want to go anyway."

At first, she'd snap, "We'll be in the car," dragging me outside. We'd swelter with the windows rolled down and the doors open. She wouldn't turn on the radio because it might run the battery down. Sometimes she considered leaving without him and started the car. Each time, he came outside with a frown, slamming the back door. We went, but no one enjoyed it.

Most days mother cleaned and cooked. She hated having me "underfoot," so she enrolled me in 4-H to learn basic skills. But she spent every mealtime telling my father that I should be inside with her. "That sun will just ruin her complexion. She'll fall off that *damn* horse and break her neck."

My father would look out the dining room window and tap his fingers on the journal beside his plate. "Right now, I need her help because I can't afford to hire a man."

Setting the table for lunch, I once complained that I couldn't learn to be a rancher if I stayed inside. She replied, "You might need something to fall back on." She stirred the gravy furiously for a minute before whipping around to face me. "And don't marry a rancher. A doctor or a lawyer would be nice, someone who can take care of you. So you won't have to work."

My fantasy summer on the ranch ended the first day I went to the local grade school. My mother wanted me to go to Rapid City, a larger town, but the thirty-mile drive was too long. Instead, I went to Hermosa, among children who had known each other since birth. One day that fall, when everyone was playing softball at recess, the batter ahead of me threw the bat over his shoulder and knocked me cold. When I came to, I quit team sports forever. Instead of offering the kind of sympathy I expected, the country kids laughed and called me a coward. I told my mother, and she reminded me of another Ogden Nash poem I'd memorized, "The Tale of Custard the Dragon."

The heroine, Belinda, practically my namesake, was a relief from the stories Mother preferred, about petite golden-haired princesses meeting handsome princes and living happily ever after. Belinda, "brave as a barrel full of bears," lived in a little white house with a black kitten named Ink and a mouse named Blink, who "chased lions down the stairs." Her yellow dog, Mustard, was "as brave as a tiger in a rage," but her pet dragon, Custard, was a coward who "cried for a nice safe cage." The other animals teased him, behavior I recognized as the same compassionate understanding I received on the playground. During the poem, Custard changed: when a pirate crawled in Belinda's window with a pistol in his hand and a cutlass in his teeth, the dragon ate him. I resolved to act brave in order to become courageous.

Modern psycho-wimps probably wouldn't approve, nor was my assimilation into schoolyard society so neatly resolved. After the oldest girl broke a raw egg on my glasses, I caved a snowbank onto her head, then ran until she caught up to me. I turned abruptly with my fist in the air and froze. She ran straight into it and got a nosebleed. After that, the girls left me alone. When an older boy pinched me as we stood in line at the front door after recess, I was able to act—I turned and socked him. His friends jeered while he clutched his handkerchief to his bloody nose. After that, the boys treated me with respectful disregard. A bit cocky, I told my parents about these battles. My father said if I got in trouble at school, he'd double whatever punishment the teacher gave me, no questions asked. Mother washed my mouth out with soap for saying the boy had pinched my "butt."

But I was still afraid of the dark and terrified these tough sons and daughters of ranchers would find out. So I decided to cure myself. After all, grownups apparently spent a lot of time out at night—I remembered mother's smile as she emerged from the darkness before she married John. By that time, my reading included James Fenimore Cooper's Leatherstocking Tales, and my new hero was my version of Natty Bumppo, the deerslayer, who walked so softly in moccasins he could sneak up on deer, so I started tiptoeing around the yard barefoot. When my father caught me at the chicken house one day, he carried me back to the house, lecturing me about kids who stepped on nails or were bitten by rattlesnakes. He bought me a pair of cowboy boots, and I seldom went outside barefoot again. I missed feeling the earth on my naked skin, but I kept practicing the deerslayer walk, putting my toes down first, until I could move quietly even in boots. Finally, on a dark night when my folks were at a community dance, I put on my boots and went outside.

Creeping through the shadows among corrals and sheds, I spent a couple of hours listening to cows breathing, their eyes shiny as they watched me. I tiptoed up the steps into the barn loft and crawled up on a roof beam. I squirmed along it until my leading hand touched something soft and warm, pigeons huddled together. One opened an eye and found my face hanging before her. She shot into the air, squawking and the flock flapped and gobbled, all trying to get through the window at once. Casually, I swung to the floor, landing on a pile of manure. I wandered toward the house, looking at stars, satisfied with my bravery.

Then came a throaty sound close as my own hair: *hoo, hoo-hoo-hoo, hoo-oo, hoo-oo.* I nearly back flipped before I recognized the call of a great horned owl. After a few moments its deep rhythm was comfortable. When the sound shifted, I followed, dazed, trying to see a shape against the stars.

Only when I blundered into a bush did I realize where I was: on the edge of a ravine clogged with willows nearly a mile from the house. It was familiar in daylight when I sneaked away from garden hoeing to bury my treasures. In the dark, the willow jungle was menacing. As I backed away, something crackled and rustled. A white-tailed doe leaped and paused between me and a rising moon. Her ears twitched. She inhaled and sprang away into the field. Walking toward the square black house, I found the darkness warm and soothing as a campfire. I've never feared darkness since.

Sonata for Horses

This afternoon, teenagers cruise the city streets with their radios turned so loud my study windows rattle to the beat. Angry and frustrated, I stare at a photograph that depicts the way I spent a lot of my childhood. I can recall details of those days: the hot pungency of horse sweat, seeing a coyote dash for cover. I can sometimes even remember lines of poetry my father quoted as we rode back and forth on the ranch. At first, we used horses for most of our trips to the pastures to check the cattle. Though my father owned a 1951 Chevy pickup, he often observed that "gas costs money," so if we could do a job on horseback, we'd saddle up.

On the August day this photograph was taken, we were riding out of the yard when Mother saw us from the kitchen window. From the back porch, she called shrilly for us to wait so that she could take our picture. She found the camera and a roll of film in the living room, shouting, "Wait!" as she came down the steps, sliding her feet to keep her bedroom slippers on. She yanked the tie on her blue quilted robe tighter. Balancing the camera on her arm, she frowned while she read the directions and loaded the film. All the while, my father's horse danced in a circle, snorting.

In the photo, Father sits erect on Zarro, his leggy Tennessee walker, reins tight because the tall horse is likely to bolt. His hat is pushed back because Mother wanted his face to show. She told him to smile, but he squints into the sun, his jaw rigid. We are wasting time.

I am riding Blaze, my first horse. I can still feel how the muscles in my thighs pulled taut when I wrapped my legs around her broad barrel. Mother wants me to lean off the horse so she can tilt my hat back and brush my hair away from my face. Responding to my father's mood, I refuse. I am not a child. I am riding my horse. I squint into the sun and try to look tough.

When Allah created the horse, he said to the wind, "I will that a creature proceed from thee. Condense thyself." And the wind condensed itself, and the result was the horse.

—MARGUERITE HENRY
King of the Wind

When my mother married John, my world expanded enormously. Instead of being the lone child of a single parent, I became part of a family enveloped in the broad acres of a grasslands ranch. As a child in the city, I'd been confined by Mother's close attention and strict rules to the narrow limits of the house. On the ranch, I revolved around my new father, following him everywhere. My life began to spin outward in ever larger circles. Mother stayed in the house. Sometimes my parents debated my future in whispers at the dinner table while I did homework in my room.

Besides space and silence, the rural community surrounded me with relatives of both parents, as well as a web of neighbors who, like my in-laws, not only knew what I did every day, but could recite my family history back several generations. I learned stories of the land and its people as I learned my father's rules. With adult eyes, I can also see how my parents' attitudes clashed.

I'd been dreaming of horses for so long that I expected to find one waiting in the barn when I woke up on my first morning on the ranch. I'd already heard tales of horsemanship from my father and his older brother, Harold. Proudly, Harold said that if the Hasselstrom boys couldn't handle a horse, nobody could. I longed to join a clan with such a reputation. My father said, "Save your money. One of these days I'll find you a horse to buy." I was disappointed but too busy following him around, listening to his stories, to mope.

Though most of our neighbors had tractors, my father used a team of workhorses to mow and rake hay the first few years. I went to the barn with him and watched as he seemed to weave the net of harness over the horses' broad backs. He wouldn't let me help. "Bud and Beauty aren't used to kids," he said. "If one of them stepped on you by mistake, it'd break your leg." When he saddled Zarro, he made me stay on the other side of the fence until he'd finished and tied the gelding in the corral, explaining, "He's so spooky he's liable to kick your head off."

So I dreamed of riding a black stallion and made secret plans. For doing my chores—gathering eggs, taking out the garbage—I earned fifty cents a week. I gave up candy and stowed every cent I made in my checking account, where Mother made me put the cash distant relatives sent on birthdays and Christmas.

At the county fair in August, I watched horses sprint past carrying kids half my age—four or five years old—while I ate dust stumbling along afoot. Determined to alter my greenhorn status, I'd already pilfered my checkbook from Mother's dresser drawer and stuffed it between my spine and the waistband of my jeans. Then as my folks examined every apron and potholder in the women's building, I escaped and bolted toward the horse stalls, shoving the checkbook into my back pocket, muttering, "I'll buy my own damn horse." The balance was nearly a hundred dollars.

That sweltering morning, I went to the horse barn and immediately spotted a "Horses for Sale" sign. I spent the next several hours dickering with a skinny man who told me to call him Mote. He kept squinting at me and blinking sweat out of his eyes.

"You're Johnny Hasselstrom's daughter?" he said when I introduced myself. "Hell, I mean heck, honey, I didn't even know he was married. Sure, you can look at my horses."

He leaned silently against the fence, elbows hooked over the top plank, while I walked to the first stall and began to stare at the horses, trying to remember what I should look for. I asked him the history, name, and price of every horse. Before I'd studied more than three, he sauntered to the water tank, filled his hat with water and dumped it over his head. He shook, swept his hair back, and replaced the hat, sighing.

I examined the horses intently, but Blaze was the only one I could afford. White hairs dappled her muzzle, but she nudged my arm sociably, and I needed all the friends I could get. While I stared at her, Mote yawned and sighed and said he'd trade the mare's rope halter and bridle for a beer.

"But Mote—Mr. Mote," I stammered, "I'm not old enough to buy you a beer." Laughing, he wiped his forehead with a black silk neckerchief, declared me a hard bargainer, and said he'd throw in the halter and bridle.

While he led the mare out, I wrote a check for eighty dollars, contemplating the attractions of a career as a horse dealer. Mote was already hurrying away when I grabbed the mare's mane to pull myself onto her back. Wrapping my legs around her well-padded ribs, I rode toward the grandstand.

Behind the sheep sheds, I met Aunt Josephine. As practice for telling my folks, I tucked a thumb in my belt and announced my news. She whooped and slapped her knee when she heard the horse trader's name. Years elapsed before I understood half the remarks Jo mumbled about him while she lifted the mare's hooves and pried her mouth open. By the time she straightened up, I knew what to look for next time I bought a horse.

Jo slapped the mare on the neck and said, "Now you can ride in the parade. I'll be lining them up in about ten minutes." She strode away, chuckling to herself, her hips jiggling in her tight pants.

My father rolled his eyes when I met him in the parking lot. As he inspected the mare, I babbled about my deal. At the big finish— that the horse trader already had my check—he shook his head and patted my shoulder. "I guess you've bought yourself a horse. We'll see about a saddle when you can stay on her." He turned toward the grandstand. I knew then that I had officially joined the scions of other ranching families, traveling properly on four legs among the wretched women and kids walking.

Next I saw my mother, wearing a thin cotton dress and high heels, buying a cold drink at the shack behind the grandstand. I clucked to the mare and was waiting when Mother turned, wobbling a bit on the uneven ground. "Hey, Mom! Look at my horse!"

She snapped her white handbag shut and looked up at me. Her blue eyes widened, and then she frowned and shook her head. "No. I told you not to ride any strange horse. Get off this instant!"

"She's mine, Mother. I just bought her. With my own money." I nudged the mare with my heel, hoping she'd prance a bit. "Her name is Blaze."

"Oh, my God," Mother said. Backing away, she looked down to check her footing. "Oh! My shoes! Damn." The white heels were stained green with manure. "You'll fall off and kill yourself." As she tottered toward the grandstand, I heard the loudspeaker announce that it was time to line up for the parade. I could already hear my aunt Jo yelling at people over by the loading chutes at the railroad tracks.

Blaze broke into a shambling trot, joining a tumult of horses carrying kids. Anyone who wanted to ride in the parade waited until Josephine, wearing a gleaming white hat and shirt with red polyester pants, motioned him or her into line. Watching as her twitchy thoroughbred mare pirouetted, I envied her graceful balance. She'd stand in the stirrups to bawl at some slowpoke. A moment later she'd flip the lines, her mare spinning away toward another knot in the parade line. For an hour, Jo was limber and willowy. At the end of the parade, she rode past the grandstand, her broad red face beaming as people applauded.

Blaze was at least fifteen years old and round as a loaf of homemade bread, her sides slick as gumbo. My father insisted I learn to ride bareback so I could learn to anticipate the horse's moves directly, through the muscles in my thighs. Mother predicted I'd be killed in several gruesome ways until Father pointed out that without stirrups, I wouldn't get my foot caught and be dragged to death. I could slide off the horse anywhere. Remounting was a problem, however. It wasn't hard at the fairgrounds, where I could lead her into a stall when no one was looking. But if I slipped or fell off in the pasture, I had to find a fence or rock—sometimes a long hike.

At the ranch, I mounted from the edge of the water tank until the time Blaze slid me off into the mud as she lay down to roll. When I was ready, I'd tap her ribs gently with my heels. She'd flip one ear and turn her great square head, rolling one eye back toward me. "Giddy up!" I'd shout, kicking her a little harder, whereupon she'd turn her head and gaze at me from the other brown eye, flapping her lips. "Move, Blaze!" I'd demand, pounding my heels against her slick barrel. Yawning, she grunted, raising her tail to eliminate excess weight in a steaming pile. Then she inhaled, spreading my thighs another six inches apart.

Meanwhile, my father would open the gate, lead Zarro out of the corral, and wait. "Hit her with the reins," he'd advise. I'd slap her hindquarters, kicking as hard as I could with both heels. As soon as her haunches cleared the gate, she would stop, and my father would have to shove her out of the way to close it.

Among the prairie swells, learning to ride from the horse's natural rhythms, I watched my father, pared to bone and sinew, leaning with every move his horse made. He stood in the stirrups when Zarro trotted, knees flexing with each jolt, spine straight and head raised. As soon as I stood so my bottom cleared the saddle, I could feel the shock of each hoof beat travel from the soles of my feet up through my thighs and hips. Instinctively, I flexed my knees and centered myself over the horse's spine, brimming with a sense of power and freedom.

While we rode, Father constantly scanned the grassland around us. A flicker at the edge of vision might draw his eye to a coyote pausing with his head and tail low before slipping out of sight. He'd gesture so I wouldn't miss the sight. Antelope made lean, racy-looking silhouettes on hilltops. Instead of running away, they dithered, stamping their front feet and whistling at us.

In June each year, we'd move the cows ten miles to summer pasture, then ride over every week to check on them and repair holes in the fence. We always went prepared for a whole day since we never knew how long the job would take. Once he learned that I was always thirsty, he started taking water along—he'd never done so when he worked alone. If I rode Blaze and Father drove the pickup, he could take more fencing tools as well as our lunch and a gallon jug of water wrapped in burlap. If we remembered to soak the burlap in a cattle tank, evaporation kept the water cool. If we both rode horses, he'd tuck sandwiches and candy bars in his saddlebags and hang a blanket-wrapped canteen on his saddle horn. Still, I got used to drinking water blood warm, spitting out pieces of hay. At first, I drank every drop we took with us before we got home. But whenever I held the jug out to my father, he refused, saying we might need it if the radiator got low. "When I was your age," he said, "we never carried water. We went all day without a drink." I learned to do the same.

The first time Blaze scraped my leg on a barbed-wire fence, ripping my jeans and slashing my thigh open, I wailed until my father rode over to look. "You'd better keep her away from the wire," he said, handing me his handkerchief. "Tie that around it. We've got work to do." The next time I got hurt, I kept silent. I discovered I could keep my face immobile by setting my jaws, but my stomach always hurt at night. "If it hurts, hide it" was a rule familiar to me long before Michael Martin Murphey sang the phrase in "Cowboy Logic."

But my father taught me more than stoicism. One day I rode over a hill to find him gently untangling a dead meadowlark from the top strand of barbed wire. He turned when he heard my horse. "Caught himself somehow, poor devil," he said. He held out the bird's corpse so I could see how the wing was torn and twisted. "Couldn't leave him just hanging there."

Like me, my mother adapted to Father's ways. How many times, I wonder, did she watch the roast dry out and the potatoes shrivel before she stopped planning for dinners on time and family outings? "Well," she'd say on the telephone, "John is so busy. We'll come if we can. Don't expect us until you see us."

———————

After a year or two of making fun of Blaze, trying to shame my father into buying me a better horse, Uncle Harold and Aunt

Josephine gave me a yearling filly. "Better take the mare, too," Harold said, shrugging. "She's too wild to keep in the corral, so I don't want her around my thoroughbreds." The mare, Donna, was carrying another colt, so in one day I acquired three new horses.

I named the little mare Rebel and started petting and gentling her at once, frustrated because my father said she wouldn't be big enough to carry my weight for at least another year. Every day I worked with Rebel—catching her, haltering and bridling her, leading her around the corrals. Murmuring endearments, I picked up each of her feet and brushed her until she was used to feeling my hands everywhere on her body. Repeatedly, I tossed an old cloth feed sack on her back and dragged it off to imitate putting on a saddle. Finally, I dragged a broken saddle out of the barn and began putting it on her back a dozen times a day. Sometimes I tied the stirrups together under her belly and left her tied in the corral for an hour or two.

While I worked at training Rebel, I began to compare her to Blaze. Rebel noticed every sound and movement, flicking her ears and rolling her eyes until I reassured her, and she learned to trust my voice. Blaze seemed to pay little attention to me, dozing even when I was riding her. Rebel not only responded to my voice and hand signals but also sometimes seemed to anticipate what I'd want her to do. The more time I spent with Rebel, the more boring poor Blaze seemed to me. When the old mare heaved herself into a plodding lope, I felt every ponderous step at the back of my head. The first time I galloped Rebel, her gait was so smooth I expected to see wings rippling behind the saddle. After months of jolting around on Blaze's broad belly, I felt light, as if I absorbed Rebel's grace by sitting on her.

By the time Rebel was two years old, my father said she was "green broke" and ready to be trained to ride. He wanted to hire a man to train her, but I argued until he nodded and said I was a natural rider. After that, when we headed over east, my father drove the pickup slowly with Blaze tied on behind. I rode Rebel to "wear her down," as father said, and get her used to the way we worked. At first, I used Blaze when I moved among the cattle, sorting some into a different pasture. If we trailed some home, for sale or treatment, I'd use Rebel and let Blaze rest, tied to the pickup as she plodded home. Before long, Rebel learned to watch the cattle more alertly than Blaze ever did. She seemed to anticipate their moves, and if a cow veered out of the herd, the horse sometimes turned so abruptly I had to grab the saddle horn to stay on.

I rode the little mare everywhere, getting her used to a variety of situations. One day I was riding with Uncle Harold to check on cows and calves in one of his pastures. His horse splashed across a gully filled with runoff from spring snows, but Rebel balked at the edge.

"What's the matter," he bawled. "Don't she like water?"

"I've never been able to get her into it," I said, kicking her in the flanks and whispering to her to quit embarrassing me.

Harold rode back and caught the reins close to Rebel's bit, gathering them into his massive hand. Then he turned his horse toward the stream again. His bulky arm stretched and bulged. Rebel leaned back and rolled her eyes, but Harold never let go. Rebel's hooves left four furrows in the mud as she slid down the bank and into the water. Then she snorted and tried to lunge to the right and left before giving up and following the pull of that big arm. Grinning over his shoulder at me, Harold hauled her twenty feet up the bank. Then he told me to turn her around and ride her back across the stream. When she balked again, he dragged her once more.

Riding on, we found the cattle Harold wanted to look over, loafing by a stock dam. Harold leaned back in the saddle, folded his hands on the horn, and said, "Now ride her in there, and let's see what she does." Rebel tossed her head and walked steadily into mud and water up to my stirrups.

Harold guffawed. "If there's anything else she don't like," he said, "just let me know and I'll drag her through that!" She never again refused to go where I wanted her to.

I think it was about that time that Mother gave me a tiny set of manicure tools in a zippered case of imitation leather. She made me sit still while she showed me how to push back my cuticles and file my fingernails. When I had a hangnail, either I couldn't find the blasted kit or I was on horseback. So I chewed my nails until they bled or whacked them short with my pocketknife.

About the time Rebel settled down, her wild red mother bore a red "horse colt"—my father's euphemism for a male. I named him Yankee. He bucked the first few times I rode him as a yearling, so my father hired a young cowboy who lived in the Badlands to break him. When I got the horse back a year later, he was terrified of everything, especially men. He bit my father and any other man who turned his back. Before Yankee quieted enough for me to bridle him alone, the young cowboy who'd ridden him was killed when a horse went over backwards, landing on top of him.

After a few summers, my father put Zarro out to pasture and began driving the pickup to the summer pasture. I followed on Rebel, who responded to my lightest message through the reins or my slight lean in the direction I wanted her to go. Yankee spent most of his time in the pasture with old Zarro until Father decided he was getting too fat. To keep "that old broomtail nag" worn down enough so he'd be quiet if we needed him, he'd tie Yankee to the back bumper of the pickup. Often, the horse simply trotted over east and back, like a dog on a leash. If we brought cattle back, I drove them with Rebel until she got tired or we ran into the neighbor's herd. Then I rode Yankee, who was fresh and ready to run.

Once as Father raced up a long hill ahead of me to open a gate, I realized I couldn't see the gelding. Dust tumbled in the pickup's wake. Yankee had fallen and Father was dragging him up the hill. I yelled and waved but couldn't get his attention, so I kicked Rebel into a run and caught the pickup just past a rocky stretch. The dust settled over Yankee, lying still.

"You've killed my horse!" I howled.

"Well, he was never much good," Father said, getting out to stand with his thumbs in his belt looking down. Yankee groaned. Father kicked him in the belly. "Get up! C'mon, get on your feet. Next time maybe you won't pull back, by God."

"You mean you knew he was down?"

"Sure. He kept pulling back, trying to break the halter or the rope. I got tired of it. The workhorses used to do that in the barn. Pull back so hard they sweenied themselves—pulled a haunch muscle."

Yankee extended his bloody front legs and tried to heave himself upright, then fell back. Dust caked both eyes. Dismounting, I tried to brush it off. Unable to see me, he jerked his head away.

"We can't have him pulling every time we tie him. Ropes are expensive," Father said behind me, "and he might get away on you when you need him."

Yankee lunged, getting his back legs under him, then stood up and shook himself. Patches of hair dangled from his ribs, scraped raw.

"Teach him a lesson once, he won't forget it," Father said, getting into the truck. He grinned at me as he shut the door. "Horses are just like kids. Got to get their attention."

Blues for Shoveling Horse Manure

As soon as I had a horse, I was free to wander alone through an immense open space of prairie. On the topographical map of the ranch, brown lines represent the high and low points of the ground, separated by tiny figures indicating elevation. When I study the map, details blur into bluebells, into a meadowlark singing on a mullein stalk, the Badlands wind smelling of clay.

A square mile on the map looks small, a cube measuring an inch on each side. The height of hills and ridges might vary by only a couple of hundred feet in that distance, but the square represents a wilderness with no fences, roads, or houses. I knew any human I saw besides my father was a trespasser to be regarded with suspicion. When I rode into a pasture to look for cattle, my father might keep watch from the pickup on top of the plateau, but I vanished from his sight at once.

I might drop down the face of a long limestone-covered slope, the horse lunging ahead while I listened for rattlesnakes. I could sideslip into a narrow ravine with rough limestone walls covered in grapevines, where a rustling under a ledge was probably a porcupine. Riding alone, I knew my horse could fall and break my leg or her own. I was alert and careful, never reaching into a place I could not see, for example, because it might hold a coiled rattler. In many of our pastures, I could observe the prairie

for four or five miles in all directions, and as far as I could see, I was the only human. I can imagine few joys greater than being alone with a good horse in such country. Perhaps this liberty created the need for solitude that made me a writer.

Once during those early years on the ranch, we took a vacation. My father was humoring my mother, before we all settled into giving the business our attention twenty-four hours a day all year. I saw the West from a sweltering cave in the car's backseat, my thighs stuck to the vinyl. Even on long windswept stretches of prairie, I usually stared out the window, smiling with joy to point out an antelope that my father missed or a hawk cruising above us.

I brought back one souvenir I still have—a framed print titled "Spirit Horse" by Woody Crumbo. When my parents tried to talk me out of buying it, I behaved as I've done ever since with things I really want. I looked once, fully, at the picture, then spun away and wandered the shop to inspect everything else. The image stayed before my eyes. I spent the rest of my hard-earned allowance to get it and no longer remember its cost. During college and graduate school, through the packing and unpacking and the many moves of my failed marriage, I lost or gave away many things—but I kept the Spirit Horse, though I rarely looked at it. Recently, as merchants concocted a craze for southwestern and native art, I unwrapped it and fell in love again.

The bright turquoise horse, dappled like an Appaloosa with white spots, stands broadside in the frame. Its white tail is carried straight up like a flag, the ends sweeping the ground—like Rebel's mane and tail when I talked my father out of hacking them short. Mane and tail swirl into a glowing white corona around the horse's entire body. Perhaps the artist meant his painting to represent the ghost of a horse, but for me it illustrated an inner fire of a horse that refuses to give up, like that of Rebel. When I rode Rebel, I saw a protective cone of light surrounding us both. I rode the prairie, free and strong. Now all my horses are dead, going back to grass on the plains. I see no aura when I walk my dog in a city park.

I have a simple philosophy. Fill what's empty. Empty what's full.
And scratch where it itches.

—ALICE ROOSEVELT LONGWORTH

One spring day when I was twelve or thirteen years old, I rode Rebel over to Uncle Harold and Aunt Jo's to see a new horse colt. Jo saw me coming from the kitchen window. "Tie your mare to that cedar post by the barn," she hollered from the back porch. "The colt's in the first stall. I'll be out when I get this cake in the oven."

When I opened the barn door, brown water poured around my boots. I ran to the house yelling, "The barn's flooded! The barn's flooded!" The screen door slapped the wall as Jo burst outside. She chucked her apron on the hood of the car and beat me to the barn.

"God, Linda. Good thing you come when you did," she said, shoving a scoop shovel under a pile of manure. "Get them horses out of here while I start this job. Water must have been running all night. Can you beat that?"

"Can you beat that?" says someone I barely hear over the oxygen's wheeze. "Josephine curled up like a baby in a bed with bars on the sides. Wouldn't that make her mad? Bet she's down to a hundred pounds."

*Against the spotless sheet, Josephine's face is dark as aged
wood, the taut tan skin crumpled. Empty pouches of skin lie
flaccid against a blue blanket. The bones of her arms stand out
as her gaunt hands clutch her shoulders.*

———

Muscles rolled in Jo's broad back. She grunted, heaving the shovel
full of manure out the door. "Take my mare first," she gasped.
The horse rolled her eyes and reared when I moved to her head.
"Princess! Cut it out!" Josephine yelled. "Tie 'em far enough apart
so they can't tangle the ropes and start kicking. Don't worry about
the work team—they're sweet. Just march ahead of 'em without
looking back." She talked and shoveled without pausing to breathe.

"Damn Harold anyway. He don't have so much on his mind he
couldn't remember to turn off a faucet. Or maybe it was that new
kid. Look at Princess shiver. Up to her knees in cold water and
horse shit. Of all the damn dumb things." *PLOP!* A shovel full of
wet horse manure struck the center of the corral.

"This kid's folks were worried about him driving around half
the night (*plop*) drinking beer. Harold said we'd put him to work.
That'd cure him. (*Plop.*) Town kids. Worthless. Never done any
work. Don't know nothing. (*PLOP!*) By the time you spend the
summer teaching them (*plop*), they want to go back to town and get
big money for working construction. (*Plop.*) Don't know nothing
about that either."

One of the workhorses rubbed his massive head against my
back, nearly knocking me down.

"Ten thousand dollars' worth of horses in this barn drowning in
(*plop*) shit. I tell you, Linda, men are the most worthless (*plop*) critters. They wear their big belt buckles and talk loud (*plop*), but there

ain't one of them worth a damn (*plop*) if some woman ain't helping them out." (*PLOP!*)

"They can't help her." My cousin shakes his head. "She hasn't said anything since I've been here. Doesn't recognize anybody."

Another cousin whispers, "Only time I can remember her ever being quiet." They cover their mouths with their hands to keep from giggling.

"The other scoop shovel's in the grain bin on that side. That kid should be shoveling this shit, not you and me. If you hadn't rode over to see that colt, I'd have missed this for another hour. I wanted to finish that cake before I did the barn chores today. Christ, this is heavy."

Finally, she leaned on the shovel. Through her damp T-shirt I saw the outline of the biggest brassiere I'd ever seen.

"What ya staring at?" She glanced down at herself and laughed. "Oh, my boulder holder's showing, eh?"

When Mother said Josephine wasn't ladylike, I suppose that's what she meant. Jo pushed her dark hair back and lifted the bottom of her T-shirt to wipe sweat off her face. A roll of soft flesh flopped over the waistband of her jeans. I looked away.

I look away, recalling the day I understood something was wrong with Josephine. She showed me pictures of her trip to

*Ireland. Harold wouldn't go with her—said a rancher had no
business taking a vacation—so she went with another woman.
She shuffled through the pictures over and over, putting down
the same ones and saying the same things. Then she clutched her
head with both hands and moaned, "It hurts so much I can't
think."*

*"Let me call Harold," I said. "Or I'll take you to the emer-
gency room."*

*"No, now sit down and eat a piece of this cake. I'll feel bet-
ter if I keep moving. I know, you haven't seen the pictures of my
trip."*

*Tubes rise out of her nose like transparent snakes, the oxygen
mask hisses. More tubes slither from the blankets to a bag of
waste under the bed. Her voice whispers in my ear, "Christ!
Ain't that the berries, me laying there with a bag of shit hanging
under me!"*

"Good. You found another shovel. Now I'm used to this kinda
work, so I'll throw my shit out the window." Jo giggled. "You
haven't got the back for that. Throw yours out the door." She
grabbed a bale of soggy straw and heaved it through the door. "I
suppose at your age you think men are terrific. You never knew
Mary Jensen. She was married to a worthless son—rascal, had a
claim down there in the breaks east of your place."

She bent and lifted the shovel again. Dark brown liquid dripped
onto her pant leg as she heaved it out the window.

"They moved down there right after they was married, had two
kids right off. Fred built a little shack, but he wasn't much account.
He'd get on his horse and say he was going hunting and wouldn't

come back for three days. She sold enough eggs to buy a cow, then she could sell milk and cream." With both of us shoveling, the rhythmic *plopping* speeded up.

"She tried to have a garden, but he hadn't dug the well very deep. If she watered the garden enough, the well'd run dry and the cow didn't have water." Jo leaned against the wall a minute to push brown curls out of her eyes. The breath rasped in her throat.

———

Breath rasps in her throat. "It can't be long now," *says an aunt.*

"*That's what the doctor's been saying for a month,*" Harold *growls.* "God, she's tough."

———

"Tough work, isn't it?" Jo heaved another shovel full out the window. "Anyway, after about three years of that, Mary caught a ride into town one day, with the kids. Fred used to call up every night on that old crank telephone of theirs, but when Harold tried to call him, no answer. Mary was staying with her folks, and she said he oughta be down there since he never went anyplace."

"So Harold rode over and looked around but couldn't find him. He come back and gathered up a few neighbors. When they got back down there, Fred's horse was standing by the house with the saddle on, starving and thirsty. Everybody was talking about maybe he just left her and the kids. Wouldn't have put it past him, but that horse made them nervous. They got the saddle off, and somebody got a bucket to get him some water. Dropped the bucket in the well and *THUMP.*" She slammed her shovel against the barn floor. I jumped.

"They thought maybe it was dry, but somebody looked down and seen a pair of shoes. One of the guys with a strong stomach rode the bucket down and got a loop around the ankles. Everybody hauled on the rope, and up come old Fred. Nobody could figure out how he come to be drowned in his own well. He'd been dead several days, maybe as long as Mary'd been gone."

She bent and thrust the shovel under another pile of soggy manure. "What are you doing, lifting that way? Use your legs, like this. Lift wrong at your age, you'll wreck your insides." *Plop.* "I've been doing this since I was ten years old. Might be why we never had no kids." *Plop.*

With full shovels, we danced around each other as the worn floorboards appeared and the barn emptied.

The room empties as relatives trade places in the death-watch, some shuffling out, others in. Do the microphones broadcast my whisper to the octagonal desk where nurses watch and listen? "Die, Josephine. You don't have to be tough any more. You've set the record."

"Some folks thought Fred killed himself, but it don't seem like a fella would dive into a well head first. Mary sold the place and bought a house in town. She did some substitute teaching, raised her kids." Josephine's laugh was shrill. "Maybe she pushed him. Nowadays women can get divorces. Help me move this feed bunk."

I squatted down, and we lifted together. "Or," Jo gasped, "they shoot the SOB and get away with it. Say he hit her. Huh. My paw never said a word to Maw without hittin' her. Said it was the only way to get her attention."

I stretched to get the kink out of my back, looking at the sun: not quite straight up. My knuckles were bleeding. We were nearly finished, so I could ride home before Mother got worried. Or maybe Jo would ask me to stay for lunch. She always made dessert.

"You know," she said, leaning her shovel against the open barn doors, "I was the oldest in our family. In the thirties, Paw took in a bunch of sheep on a debt, with no pasture. He'd get in the Model A and go to town and be gone a week. Forgot about Maw and us kids. So I started taking them sheep out along the road, letting them graze the ditches."

She started toward the house, and I followed. "One afternoon I got to looking at the neighbor's pasture. Nothing in it, and he lived forty miles away. So I started turning our sheep in there. Let them in every night and drove them back to our pasture just before sunrise. Got up in the middle of the night all summer."

"Sometimes she wakes up in the middle of the night and tries to say something," Harold said, turning his wheelchair toward the door. "But I can't understand her. You coming down to eat with us?"

"I'll stay here until you come back so she's not alone."

After he rolls into the elevator, I whisper, "I read your grandfather's journals, Josephine. When you were born, he wrote, 'The baby has a tumor on its head.' Maybe it was there all these years, waiting. Remember when I told you about my migraines? You said you never had headaches, like they were something to be ashamed of, like being lazy."

The oxygen mask collapses against her nose. I pause, expecting her to speak. "I hated you for a while, when you said I wasn't really a Hasselstrom because I'm adopted. I'm sorry. It's all right now." No answer. "I love you, Jo." The door opens as another cousin enters.

———

Josephine opened the door to the porch. "Come right on in. I scoop the dirt out about once a week. Take them filthy jeans off. I've got a pair here somewhere that will fit you. We'll throw yours in the washer, and your mom'll never know you been shoveling shit." She laughed, mouth wide open, her big white teeth reminding me of the horses. Yanking open a cupboard, she tugged a stack of faded jeans and shirts out onto the floor. "Take your pick."

She jerked her shirt off over her head. "God! There's even horse shit in my bra!" Laughing, she unsnapped it. Her massive breasts swung free. "Shut your mouth before you get flies in it. Ain't you ever seen tits before?"

Mother always shut the bedroom door when she dressed. I turned to scramble through the pile of jeans.

"I guess not."

When I found a pair that fit, I undressed with my back to Jo and stepped into them. They caught on my hipbones and stayed put.

Jo pulled a T-shirt over her head and laughed. "Anyway, I spent the whole summer sneaking those sheep around the countryside at night. Every now and then, Paw would see them and say how amazing sheep were, to get that fat on that old dusty pasture. Come fall, I got a neighbor to haul them to town and brought the money back to Maw. Don't know what we'd have done without it, and Paw never did figure it out."

She used both heavy hands to comb her limp hair back on her skull and turned toward the kitchen. "Smells like the cake's done. I don't think we're going to cut that little horse colt. He looks like he's hung well enough to make a stud. Maybe when he's old enough, we can put him with that Rebel mare we give you."

In the kitchen, she yanked a cake out of the oven and clanged it down on the counter. "Ain't that little stud got the cutest little do-whopper you ever saw? Guess you haven't seen too many." She shook her hand and stuck her burned fingers in her mouth. "Ouch, dammit! Anyway, that's the best one I've seen in a while. Spend more time looking at horses' dicks and less at the men's, we'd all be better off." She opened a cupboard and scattered plates on the table. "Here comes Harold, and dinner's ready. I'll call your maw while you wash your hands."

I cup my hands around Jo's naked head, warm as a loaf of new bread, and kiss her temple. "God, Josephine, you looked fine on that racy mare. I'm going home now, and I won't be back. Next time they call us to come up here to watch you die, I'm going to saddle a horse and ride out."

Reckoning the Cost of a Dead Steer

I've opened all the windows on the second floor of the house to let the wind blow through, too hot for May and carrying car exhaust so thick I can almost see it. Out in the street, brakes squeal and an angry male voice yells, "Where did you learn to drive, lady?"

Sitting at my computer, I grin, wondering if the woman learned where I did—in pastures with no traffic lights, no competing cars, no drivers with cell phones at their ears yelling at her. My father started teaching me to drive when I was nine, letting me steer the pickup while he pitched hay off the back. I practiced in the hayfields and pastures as we worked. At that time, a South Dakota resident could get a driving license at fourteen, so in the spring of 1956, my father began reviewing driving rules as we drove, creating challenges to prepare me for the risks of driving on the highway. I failed a quiz on brakes just before my fourteenth birthday.

My father told me to drive him to the summer pasture. At the second gate, I couldn't find the brake pedal. I forgot about turning off the ignition and stomped on the gas pedal. All the while he sat utterly still. The gate wire sang as the pickup lurched through it. Then the top wire popped and the broken end ricocheted off the windshield like a bullet. He didn't duck.

He kept silent while he helped me untangle the wire from the front bumper. From the back of the truck, he took the wire stretcher, a little coil of new wire, and the fencing tools. Then he got in the driver's seat and said, "I'll be back when I finish checking the cows." I stared after the pickup as it disappeared over a low rise a mile off. Its speed never slackened. The sound of the motor drained into a breeze.

By then, I'd ridden my horse alone through the same pastures for five years, but I turned in a circle, staring as if I'd landed on a distant planet. Five miles west, near the faint blue line of the Black Hills, lay a highway and the ranch house where my mother was washing clothes, unaware that my father had abandoned me.

On the east the fence crossed a plowed field to disappear toward jagged pink Badlands peaks sixty miles away. The summer pasture was eight miles away, so even if the cattle were all right, he wouldn't be back for two hours.

My eyes were wet, but my mouth was dry. He hadn't left the water jug, but a dipper hung from a windmill a half mile away. At least I wouldn't die of thirst.

I sighed and said to a meadowlark singing on a post, "Tore hell out of that gate." I wasn't allowed to swear around my folks.

When my father came back, the gate stood tight and strong. I hadn't been more scared than I could handle. After the job was done, I'd walked to the tank for a drink and washed tear tracks from my dusty face. Now I leaned against the gatepost, chewing nonchalantly on a piece of grass. Silently, my father slid to the passenger side, and I drove back to the ranch.

The shell is America's most active contribution to the formation of
character. A tough hide. Grow it early.

—ANAÏS NIN
The Diary of Anaïs Nin

The summer I turned fourteen, I developed into a tangle of hor-
mones and growing muscles. Even my body was rebelling against
my mother's plans for a delicate, ladylike daughter. I was already
taller than she was, and my feet had been larger since I was ten years
old. Adulthood was so close I could inhale its musky perfume and
dream of running my fingers through its hair. My father often
reminded me that in his youth, both men and women were considered adults at ten or twelve years of age, but he still called me Child
instead of using my name.

My birthday was in the middle of haying season, so we were all
usually too busy to have a party. On every normal summer day, after
breakfast at six, I mowed and raked hay while my father stacked.
About mid-morning, we stopped in the field. Father drank coffee
while I drank water and checked the bolts on my mower and rake.
With a grease gun, I squeezed lubricant into zerks, nipple-like grease
fittings leading to moving joints. Mother worked in the garden during the cooler mornings and brought lunch to the field around one
o'clock. After she left, we lay down in the shade of a stack, heads on
our jackets. Sometimes we napped until two. We quit work at dark,
about nine, and ate cold sliced beef and salad for supper.

I loved the muscles growing on my skinny arms as I worked and
sweated, sang songs, and felt myself growing up. The blood croon-
ing through my body promised adventure. I loved my tractor, the
danger and rhythm of the work. Daydreaming about a wonderful
adulthood, I slid my hands over my body and imagined how good
I'd be at adult stuff, like sex.

On the morning of my fourteenth birthday, Mother made a little speech about what a milestone this was: I was becoming a woman. "I think you ought to quit early and relax a little before supper. And we'll have birthday cake and ice cream for dessert." My father nodded without committing himself, but I hoped we'd shut off the tractors at seven. "Chocolate cake, please," I reminded her. Father made his annual promise that on the next rainy day—when we couldn't cut hay or work cattle—we could do anything I wanted. I always chose to go to the Black Hills. I loved walking on pine needles in dim, quiet aisles between the trees. I loved listening to singing streams, picking new wildflowers to identify. The trip was always such a joyous contrast to the ranch, where the only water lay in muddy stock dams, the ground was cracked and dry, and the wildflowers tended to be prickly.

After supper and pink angel food cake from a mix, Mother brought out her presents, work socks and shirts in colors I didn't like. "They were on sale," she said. We sat at the dining room table while I unwrapped everything, trying to be grateful. Father tapped his fingers on the oilcloth while Mother refolded the wrapping paper, some of it printed with Christmas trees and snowmen, or pink bunnies. "This paper is older than you are, dear," she said.

When Father put the paper in the high cupboard for her, he opened the one next to it, where he kept an old .22 rifle. I expected him to get down a new horse blanket because my old one was worn so small it barely covered the horse's back. Instead, he brought out a gift I hadn't dared to hope for: a .22 rifle.

"Now, I bought this box of shells," he said, handing it to me with his tight little smile, "but from now on you buy your own, out of your allowance."

"Oh, you bet," I breathed. "Can we go over to the prairie dog town and try her out?" I knew even then that guns and other lethal weapons are always called "her," although I didn't know why.

"Right now?" he said, glancing at my mother. "I guess it's still light enough." Mother frowned and said, "Don't shoot yourself in the eye."

We went. Father helped me load it the first time with .22 long rifle bullets, saying I should never use anything else. He told me to put it down before I climbed through a fence and to leave an empty chamber, only that didn't apply to this rifle because it was a pump. As I jacked a new shell into the firing chamber, the old one was automatically ejected, fast and smooth. That first night I got five prairie dogs with eight shots.

My father shook his head and said he couldn't have done any better. All he ever used his rifle for was shooting skunks that got into the chicken house, or knocking off stray tomcats in the spring. Some guinea hens took up residence at our place once, and their squawking every morning drove him out with the gun, but it took him a long time to kill the last of them.

After that, I saved my money and bought a used scabbard to buckle onto my saddle and took the .22 with me everywhere. When Mother pursed her lips, Father shook his head at her. After I cut the prairie dog population, I shot three cottontail rabbits one day. Mother made me skin them and said the new rule was that I eat anything I shot.

My father approved. I got pretty good at skinning rabbits until I counted thirty in the freezer and realized I was sick of rabbit stew. I considered bringing Mother a prairie dog, but when I picked it up, forty fleas ran up my arm. I stopped shooting everything I saw.

But I still carried the rifle when I went riding and sometimes shot at posts or old pieces of wood just to improve my aim. I got very, very good, but because I was an only child and seldom saw the neighbor kids, no one else knew. I daydreamed about making impossible shots to save my father from a rattlesnake bite or my mother from a drunken burglar.

That winter, just before Christmas, my parents decided that I was old enough to stay alone for a few days while they took a short trip. They left me lists of instructions about the cattle, phone numbers to call if I needed help, notes about watering the plants. By the time they drove away, I had stopped listening to their directions, so they leaned out the car windows to repeat the important things: Don't use the rifle. Don't ride the horse. Don't drive on the highway.

"And if it snows, darling," my mother said, "call your Uncle Harold to come do the chores. I don't want you to freeze to death." She always worried about things that wouldn't happen. I never mentioned the real dangers, like getting kicked while I was feeding.

That morning, I did the regular chores: scattered grain for the chickens, pitched hay to the milk cow and my horse, and grained the bunch of steers we'd sell next spring. I really enjoyed feeding things. The chickens clucked when I came and let me scratch their backs. The steers ate pieces of cattle cake out of my hands, wrapping their long tongues around my fingers to suck up the sweet blocks without biting. As long as I moved slowly and talked quietly, they stayed close, licking my pant legs, nibbling at my pockets, their big brown eyes making them look like astonished children.

I took my time doing chores, thinking that if the folks had forgotten anything, they'd be back within an hour. Carefully, I examined the steers, because it was the right time of year for waterbelly.

Minerals that plug the urinary canal of a steer—a castrated male—cause waterbelly. My father explained it to me in high-flown language, but I heard the vet use simpler terms. A waterbelly steer can't pee. If he's not treated, his bladder fills and breaks, and his own urine poisons him. If the condition is caught in time, the vet digs into the flesh of his haunch below his anus, finds the urinary tube, pulls it outside the hide and sews it down. Because the urine drains at the rear, vets call it "turning him into a heifer." The operation might save the steer's life, but he won't bring as much at the sale ring. To prevent waterbelly, we fed the steers salt, so they would drink enough water to wash the minerals out of their system.

I walked slowly around each steer studying the shape of his belly and watching for any that were switching their tails more than usual.

When I was sure my folks weren't coming back, I dug through the tractor repair manuals in my dad's shop until I found a magazine with pictures of naked women. I studied it awhile, catching up on fine points of anatomy. Then I gathered up the notes my folks had left all over the house and sat at the kitchen table to read them. They hadn't left much room for initiative. One of Mother's said, "Clean your room," and when I saw Father's list headed, "Things to do if you run out of things to do," I knew why he'd been chuckling to himself after dinner the night before: "Shovel manure out of the barn. Clean the chicken house."

For four days, I sang while I did the chores and still had time to study and clean my room. I shoveled out the chicken house, then dug out the old nesting material and replaced it with fresh straw, something neither of them had thought to mention. I considered breaking a rule by inviting some friends over, but a two-day blizzard saved me from temptation. I shoveled new paths to the garage, the chicken house, and the barn every morning.

Late in the afternoon of the sixth day, feeding the steers in the evening, I realized I was one short, the one that always licked my hip pockets until I fed him a piece of cake. I plodded over the only hill in the pasture and found him lying in the corner of the corral, switching his tail like the director of a marching band. His eyes were dull. I kicked him in the flank to get him up, but he just stared at me. "Damn. Hell. Jesus Christ. Crap," I yelled. He struggled to his feet.

His belly hung almost to the ground, grotesquely swollen. His bladder had burst. For all practical purposes, he was a dead steer, but he might walk around for days.

I went back to the house to fix supper and think. The job was simple, just like the day Father threw the fencing tools on the ground before he disappeared over the horizon. A vet wouldn't save the steer, only bill us for seventy-five dollars. My folks were due back in a few days, and the steer might still be alive then, but he'd suffer. If my dad were here, he'd "put the poor critter out of his misery." But I wasn't supposed to shoot the rifle.

All evening I picked up books, read a little and threw them down, wishing I'd found the steer sooner. The livestock paper beside my father's chair announced that nine-hundred-pound Hereford steers were cheap that year, selling for $20.10 per hundred pounds. He was worth nearly two hundred dollars. That meant my allowance for four years if I had to pay for him.

In the morning, I managed to cook two eggs without breaking the yolks, then did chores in the usual order: fed and watered the chickens, milked the cow, fed the horse. I dumped buckets of grain in the feed bunks without looking at the steers, then counted them. One short.

Over the hill, he was lying in the same spot, head down. His breathing was irregular. I swore at him until he moved ahead of me down the hill and into a corral. Too large for what I had to do, it was the only pen with a gate wide enough for the pickup. I'd need to back up close.

In the house, I loaded my .22. I had only ten bullets. Back in the corral, the steer stood, tail switching, his belly dragging in the snow. I leaned across the top rail of the fence, inhaled, and sighted on his left eye. I'd never shot anything larger than a rabbit but imagined the principle was to hit a vital spot. I always hit prairie dogs in the eye.

The first shot sounded like the wet slap the dishrag made when I swatted a fly. The steer shook his head and bellered. I jacked in another shell and pulled the trigger. Missed.

Faster, because he was shaking his head and bawling, I fired again, into his neck.

He swung his head and started to trot and I kept aiming and firing. Blood was trickling out of his eye, nose, and neck. He was trotting, staggering around the corral, bawling and bumping into posts on his blind side.

I waited until he turned toward me, sighted on his chest and fired three times before I heard a click: out of bullets.

The steer's left eye was only a pulpy hole in his skull. He ran and stumbled, spraying blood. I was crying hard, blinded. My hands shook as I groped in my pockets. No bullets.

I stumbled to the house and found an old box of .22 short rifle bullets in my father's gun cupboard. He told me shooting anything but .22 longs might ruin my rifle. I never thought of using his rifle.

"I don't have any choice," I sobbed as if someone cared. "I just don't have any choice." I fumbled with the shells, hoping the steer would be dead before I got back.

He was standing on the far side of the corral, turning his head, trying to see everything out of one good eye, trying to be ready to charge whatever was hurting him, smash it with his heavy head. But he couldn't see anything to chase.

Agitated by the blood smell, the other steers were pushing at the fence, roaring and pawing dirt. As I walked toward the corral, the steer bawled and turned his eye toward me. This time I had to get close since the .22 shorts had less power. I opened the gate and pulled it shut without fastening it, in case I needed to get out fast.

The steer was facing me, but I didn't want to shoot him in the forehead, where the skull was thicker. I waved, and he jumped sideways, looking toward the other steers. I pumped three bullets into his ear as fast as I could. He stood moaning, and then his knees buckled.

Kneeling in the snow, he stared straight ahead but wouldn't fall. He groaned hoarsely, continuously. The other steers screamed and ran back and forth by the fence, snuffling and blowing.

I sighted on the spot behind the shoulder where his heart was and stepped forward. One step. Two. Three. Four. The rifle muzzle nearly touched his shoulder, and still the steer didn't move. Bloody froth bubbled out of his nostrils.

I fired. Again. Again. I could hardly work the lever action. The shells were fouling the gun, maybe ruining my beautiful rifle.

Again. Again. The steer moaned and coughed blood on the snow. When he toppled, his head struck my foot. Blood poured out of his side and around my boots. His good eye grew dull, like a lead marble. He sighed and was still. Heat from his body warmed my face, manure pooled under his tail.

I knelt in the blood, put my face against his neck, and sobbed until I was dry inside, swearing to the steer that I'd never be so clumsy again.

———

The memory of shooting the steer still unnerves me, but beside it rises another memory. On a winter day a couple of years ago, my father and I went to the barn to load cattle cake for feeding and found dozens of fifty-pound paper sacks of cattle cubes ripped open. Thousands of cubes, easily a hundred dollars' worth of winter feed, were scattered and covered with excrement and urine.

"Badger's work," said my father grimly. "Might as well shovel it into the garbage. A cow won't eat that junk."

"I'll put it on my garden," I said. "Good mulch. But I don't think a badger made this mess." A badger is powerful enough—a twenty-five-pound badger no bigger than a beagle is stocky and bowlegged as a weight lifter. But I didn't believe the destruction fit a badger's tidy habits. After we fed the cows, my father got a hammer and a few old boards and went around the barn trying to cover holes while I shoveled the ruined cake into a wheelbarrow and dumped it on my garden plot.

The next morning, another dozen sacks were ruined. "I think it's hopeless," my father said. "A badger could tear that barn down if he wanted in." I still disagreed, but I kept my mouth shut. That night I crept to the barn at midnight with my .22 rifle. When I snapped on the flashlight and opened the door of the feed storage room, a huge raccoon turned to face me. I fired twice and waited until the body stopped twitching, then went back to bed. In the morning, I dragged the corpse outside just as my father arrived. "What happened?"

"I shot a coon last night. But she's a nursing female. She probably has a dozen kits stashed in here somewhere."

"I hope they starve to death," he growled. "At least she won't be feeding them cake every night."

I returned to the barn with the rifle about midnight. This time when I shone the light inside, three tiny goggle-eyed faces turned toward me—baby raccoons. One by one, they put their paws over their eyes. I groaned, but shot them anyway. Having learned to scavenge, to forage destructively in human storage areas, they would never go back to hunting their own natural nourishment. In the same way, learning how to kill more efficiently had seasoned me, and I could never erase the knowledge.

Lightning Strikes
the White Heifer

*The sun looked fragile this June morning, hanging high over the city
behind thin clouds, but I took my coffee to the back steps and tipped my
face up to heat that was mostly imaginary.*

*Frodo squeezed his sturdy West Highland white terrier posterior onto
the top step where I sat, nudging me until I massaged the spot between
his shoulder blades. Two robins fluttered back and forth from their nest
in the apple tree to the electric pole in the alley, squawking. Then a shadow
slid over the grass. Looking up, I recognized one of the most beautiful
grasslands predators, a red-tailed hawk. I watch for their heart-shaped
silhouettes on fence posts when I drive back and forth to the ranch.*

*The hawk perched on the top of the pole, folded its wings and leaned
forward, turning its head to scrutinize the yard with first one eye, then
the other. The robins shrieked and flew in faster circles. Then the hawk
dropped, skimmed between the branches of the apple tree and plucked a
half-grown chick from the robins' nest. The chick squealed as the hawk
swept once across the yard, gaining altitude, then surged out of sight over
an eighty-foot cottonwood. The robins pursued, screeching, for a block or
two before turning back.*

*I leapt to my feet, cheering for the hawk. She is learning to live in
the city, practicing her inborn hunting skills above the tidy lawns and*

broken asphalt. If she can adapt, perhaps I can too. I straightened my
spine, drained my coffee cup, and went inside, determined to view my life
as only another challenge, a chance to discover once more what I am.

I believe a leaf of grass is no less than the journey-work of the stars,
And the pismire is equally perfect, and a grain of sand, and the egg
    of the wren,
And the tree-toad is a chef-d'oeuvre for the highest,
And the running blackberry would adorn the parlors of heaven,
And the narrowest hinge in my hand puts to scorn all machinery,
And the cow crunching with depress'd head surpasses any statue,
And a mouse is miracle enough to stagger sextillions of infidels.

                    —Walt Whitman
                     "Song of Myself"

Last week, I made the five-hour drive to the ranch on Thursday
afternoon to keep a Friday morning appointment with my doctor in
Rapid City. Neither of my parents was home when I stopped at their
house, so I wrote a note about my appointment and taped it to the
edge of the kitchen sink, where they'd be sure to see it.

    I ate breakfast on the porch of my ranch house the next morn-
ing, soaking up heat reflected from the siding and listening to the
blackbirds. When I heard cows bawling, I looked down at the corrals and saw that my father had shut twenty cows in the corral and
was lighting a fire. Maybe he'd gotten someone to help him brand, I
thought. All this rainy spring, the corrals were a muddy mire. Some
ranchers began making plans to brand new calves early in April,

calling the neighbors who trade the chore among them until everyone has finished. Each time they had to cancel because of the contin-
uous rain. Water soaked so deeply into the churned-up ground in
the corrals that horses, calves, and people would slip and fall.
Working in the mud is irritating and dangerous, and a hot branding
iron laid on wet hair can create a blistered brand that becomes
infected.

I'd just stepped inside to get my purse, ready to head for my
doctor's office, when the phone rang. "Are you gonna get down here
before noon so we can get these calves branded?" my father barked.

I explained to him about my appointment, but my choice was
simple. If I left, he would try to brand the calves alone. By the time I
called the doctor to cancel and got to the corral, my father had roped
a calf and was trying to drag it to the branding table.

That night, sitting in a tub of hot water, I studied the bruises on
my thighs where calves had kicked me, telling myself I should not
have changed my plans. I breathed deeply, pushing away the pain in
my knee, the one in which all the ligaments had torn loose a few
years before when my horse stepped on it. What would I have done,
though, if I'd come home and found my father dead?

My father and I struggled to brand another twenty calves the
next day before I fled back to the city. A couple of days later, he
called me in Cheyenne for the first time. We had to brand the rest of
the calves, he said—they were already fifty to a hundred pounds
heavier than they usually are when we handle them, so the job
would be harder and more risky. We couldn't wait any longer, and
we didn't dare turn them into the summer pasture without our
mark of ownership because somebody had been stealing calves in the
neighborhood.

I was ready to argue that the two of us could not do the job
alone when he beat me to it. "An old man and a crippled girl can't

do the job alone," he said. "If you get a crew together for next week-end, I'll just leave the job to you. The rain's going to stop, so the corrals will be dry."

Trusting his dependable weather sense, I called friends, hoping my father had realized that he and I must work out some compromise for managing ranch work.

The sun had shone every day during the past week, and when I got to the ranch, I checked the corrals. The ground was baked hard and dry.

Early the next morning, I went down to my parents' house to plan the day with my father and gather supplies. Mother told me he'd finished breakfast an hour before and gone somewhere, adding, "I hope you aren't planning on me cooking lunch for any branding crew. I'm going shopping."

I carried equipment from the barn to the corral, replacing bent hypodermic needles and old castrating bands with new ones bought in Cheyenne. I found the outdated vaccine my father had stored in the cellar, stashed it in my car to dispose of later, and arranged the new bottles close to the branding chute. I hung ropes on several posts, so we could easily catch a calf that tried to turn back. Next to the propane tank that fueled the fire, I placed the branding irons and the horn irons with concave ends in graduated sizes. Red hot, these burn the calves' horns down to the roots, a less painful method than waiting until the horns grow and cutting them off. The heat also cauterizes the horn base, preventing infection.

Everyone had arrived and gathered in the corral by the time my father appeared. On a normal branding day, he'd have helped me organize, telling stories about past branding days, looking over the calves and reminding me which cows had produced the healthiest offspring. This morning, he looked around the circle twice, his smile growing stiff as he realized my volunteers were all women. Then he

shook hands with everyone and told me shortly to place my brand
on five steers. Usually, I branded five steers to sell and five heifers to
keep as I gradually built my own herd.

"I hope none of your little girlfriends get hurt and sues us," he
said turning away. "We could lose the ranch." Stumbling a little over
the ruts in the corral, he walked off. I took a picture of him, the last
on a roll of film.

My women friends were all artists, and several had ranch back-
grounds or had helped me brand before, so most of them knew what
to do. We traded jobs back and forth, helping each other, discussing
the arts we practiced, and talking of the changes in our lives since
we'd seen each other last. I suggested they all add "branding" to the
list of skills on their résumés.

For the first time in my life, I handled the branding irons alone.
Every previous year, either my father did the job, or he handed the
irons to any male who happened to be helping, even if he'd never set
foot on a ranch before. Both my husbands branded calves ineptly,
raising blisters, cutting tender skin with the sharp edges of the
homemade irons. Now I proved I'd learned how to do it right by
watching all those years.

Castrating is another job my father never let me do. Until I was
fourteen, he made me leave the corral while he sliced open a calf's
testicles and removed the sperm sacs—even if he and I were the
entire branding crew. After I'd helped brand on several other
ranches, I simply refused to leave. He shrugged and kept cutting,
but he never let me do it, even after we stopped using the knife. When
I married George, Father left us alone the first spring to do the branding. George always kept his knife sharp, but he grew up on a cherry
farm in Michigan, so I had to show him how to do the job. "I used
to think ranching would be fun," he mumbled as he sliced a hair-
covered sac, "but at least we didn't have to castrate cherry trees."

This spring, the bull calves were still young enough that we could place especially heavy rubber bands around the cord leading to the sperm sac to cut off the blood supply so the testicles shrivel, dry, and drop off without bloodshed.

"Which is it?" I asked as a singer pushed a calf into the chute.

She lifted a calf's tail. "Tell me the difference again."

"One hole means it's a bull, which we'll turn into a steer. Two-holers are female."

"Just like real life," said the weaver. "This one has one hole."

When the singer said, "Your turn," and handed the weaver the castrating bands, she protested. "I don't need to know how to castrate."

"Do you date men?" someone asked. She nodded. "Then it might come in handy." With another feminist my age, I made up jokes about "castrating females," but we had to explain to the younger women how the term is used to belittle strong women.

We finished branding all seventy calves by noon, and the women helped me tote the branding supplies back to the barn. Working with the traditional male branding crew, I cleaned up alone while the men leaned on their pickups and talked. Then they followed me to the house, where I fed them roast beef and potatoes put into the oven at dawn. For dessert, they expected pies and cakes baked earlier.

Instead, I'd asked each woman to bring a potluck dish. While some of us washed our hands and faces, comparing wounds and covering them with iodine and bandages, others arranged the meal on the table. Tradition would demand that we haul chairs from every corner of my house to crowd around the table in my small dining room. Instead, we filled our plates—mostly salads—and sat on the living room floor. The smell of burning calf hair and fresh manure permeated our clothes, mingling with the odor of hand lotions and herbs. We laughed a lot.

By two P.M., clouds were boiling up in the west, spilling over the Black Hills like suds out of a washing machine. The women looked at their watches, hastily hugged each other, and sprinted for their cars, ducking as lightning bolts struck the hill south of the house. While I watched the news, lightning struck the antenna on top of a thirty-foot pole lashed to the deck. Showering sparks threw a white glare in the rattling windows and flame squirted out of a living room outlet. I unplugged the television and watched the genuine weather news, presented by experts. Blue bolts slammed into hilltops and seemed to stick there, quivering like spears. Thunder shook the house.

An inch of rain pelted down, turning dry gullies to white froth for fifteen minutes. As the clouds moved east and the downpour eased, I waded outside with a fresh roll of film in the camera. The day's last weak sun rays fell on a two-hundred-pound Charolais heifer calf lying a little too still near her grazing mother. Pure white as an Old Testament sacrifice, she was unmarked except for the bloody ear notch washed clean by the rain and the black brand I'd put on her three hours before. Struck dead by lightning.

"Thanks," I said to the rain gods. Ranchers often behave as if we have to pay for good luck, so the calf was our sacrifice in return for the spring rains.

When I woke at dawn, six vultures robed in priestly black had gathered on the corpse to collect the offering. Briefly, I considered interpreting the sight as an omen, the scavengers lining up to devour the ranch as my parents' faculties failed.

At sunrise, I walked through the branded calves, checking to see that none was scratching the new brand or bleeding from an ear notch, brand, or horn wound. The cows' udders had all been sucked, and most of the calves were lying on a sunny slope, bellies full.

When I told my father about the dead calf, he only nodded and asked me to go over east with him to check the fences in the summer pasture.

I was surprised to see a dozen dry cows—ones that hadn't calved in the spring. Usually, my father kept them close to home, ready to sell. They were gathered in the big dam, where thick black soup sucked at their bellies as they sipped clear water off the top.

Driving back to the ranch, we didn't hold our usual conversation. Ordinarily, he'd remark how low the water was for June. I'd say the calves were looking good, though. He'd look at me out of the corner of one eye and say with a grin, "Drinking that mud makes 'em put on weight faster." Then we'd laugh and agree it was time to move them to the next pasture, where a good spring fills the dugout even in a dry year.

Instead, we rode in silence. I couldn't imagine how my father would keep track of the cows without me. Nor could I consider moving back to my house on the hill to be hired labor—watching his body and mind deteriorate. My father detoured from our usual route and pulled up at a neighbor's gate that was always too tight for me to open. This time I released it easily, noticing how my father had spliced the top two wires to make it looser.

He drove without speaking until he pulled up in front of the garage and turned off the ignition. "Going back to Cheyenne tomorrow?"

I nodded, already dreading my next trip back to the ranch. Inside my house, the air reeked of burning hair. I opened all the windows and set a fan at the open door, facing out. I ate a sandwich in front of the late news and settled in George's chair. I was slitting open the top letter on the bag of mail Mother had collected for me during the week when the phone rang.

"Your father had a little trouble in the bathroom," my mother said. "He's not feeling very well. Could you come down? But don't tell him I called you."

When I pulled open the back screen door at my parents' house, Mother was holding the inner door half open. She leaned around it to whisper, "He's lying on the dining room floor and says he's comfortable now. There's no sense in you bothering him. I'll talk to you in the morning." She put her shoulder against the door, trying to close it. With both hands I pushed back, hearing my mother's bedroom slippers slide across the floor, surprised at how light she was, how easily I could move her. I glanced in the bathroom. Gouts of blood blotched the gray linoleum floor, a bloody hand print marred the pink wall.

My father was stretched out in the dining room just outside the bathroom door. Grizzled hair flared around his face. His belt was unbuckled and his pants unzipped. One bedroom slipper was missing, and his naked foot shone white as porcelain with vivid blue veins. I sat down to take his cold hand and felt a vein writhe slowly under my index finger. I brushed a lock of straight black and white hair away from his nose and saw blood smeared beneath it. Veins pulsed in his temples and white forehead.

"I thought I'd lay here awhile, till I feel better," he said without opening his eyes. "I vomited. Must have been something I ate."

Behind me, I heard Mother wiping the plastic tablecloth on the round oak table. "He didn't eat much for supper," she murmured. That reminds me, I need potatoes." She turned to the refrigerator and started to scribble on her grocery list. "Darn pen!" She threw it in a drawer and reached for another.

"I only know," my father said, quoting a favorite line, "that summer sang in me / A little while, that in me sings no more."

I studied his face. Was he delirious? "Mother, why don't you sit here with him while I call the ambulance?" I said over my shoulder. At the buffet, she was pulling pens from an overflowing drawer to try them on scraps of paper before tossing them back.

"No ambulance," Father croaked, shaking his head. "No hospital." I knew why he didn't want to go, remembering a night when I was thirteen. He'd complained that his stomach hurt, but he insisted my mother take me to a 4-H dance. By midnight, when he finally asked me to drive them both to the hospital, his appendix had ruptured. While he recovered, he told me about waking up in the hospital when he had rheumatic fever. Everyone was standing around the bed, he said, waiting for him to die. He never wanted to go to another hospital.

"You need help," I said. "You've lost a lot of blood. Would you rather ride in my car? I've got blankets so it would be just like lying here."

He snatched his hand out of mine. "You're not taking me anyplace. I'm going to lay right here on my own dining room floor and rest. Like I've always said, 'This above all: to thine own self be true.'"

My father always had a quote to suit every incident, so our conversation seemed almost normal. "I'll back the car up to the door," I said, standing up, "so you won't have to walk far." Water was running in the bathroom, and I found Mother filling a plastic pail in the sink while she brushed her teeth. "I've got to clean this up before it dries," she said. "Bloodstains are so hard to get out."

"I'll do it." I found a sponge and several rags under the sink. "You get warm clothes and your coat and ride with us to the hospital."

She frowned. "He doesn't want to go. You know how difficult he can be."

"He's lost too much blood to think straight." I squeezed out the sponge, then dipped it in the blood on the floor and wrung it over the toilet. Thick red gobs lay behind the stool and on the hand towels on the rack. *Who would have thought the old man to have so much blood in him?* Said my damned brain, quoting Shakespeare out of long habit.

No time. I dropped the sponge and ran outside to back my car close to the steps. By the time I spread blankets in the cargo area of my Bronco and went back inside, my hands were shaking. Mother stood in the kitchen wearing her faded bathrobe and flannel pajamas.

"I'm going to bed, dear," she whispered. "I put a blanket over your father so he'll stay warm. Maybe in the morning I'll try to locate a doctor in Rapid City. You know, we've been having check-ups at the Mayo Clinic, so we haven't been to a doctor here in years. In fact, maybe we should just call Mayo's. We could proba-bly get in there in three weeks or so." She scribbled a note on her blackboard—would she forget otherwise?—and snapped off the kitchen light.

I stood by the telephone, listening to her slippers slide toward the bedroom. Even in the dim light from the dining room, I could see grime around the cupboard handles. I used to tease her by saying that her shelves held the world's largest collection of plastic contain-ers from fake whipped cream. One deep drawer below the counter bulged with plastic bags she washed and dried to reuse. Another drawer contained dozens of half-burned candles, stray jar lids, and Currier and Ives prints cut from old insurance company calendars. My grandmother's bread pans and a hand-cranked cream separator, furry with dust, lay on the top shelf with antique spices and two butter churns. In a shallow drawer next to the phone, dry pens rat-tled among squares of paper mother cut from advertising circulars to use for notes and grocery lists. Later, when I am cleaning her house and throwing useless junk away, I find a shoebox on the top shelf of her bedroom closet stuffed with notes written by my father. Some are mundane, like "Wife, I've gone over east." Others are more lyrical: "My love, how about breakfast in town? John."

Dialing the sheriff's number, I gave directions to the dispatcher. "Be sure," I repeated, "you don't go to Harold Hasselstrom's. That's my uncle. He's been having heart trouble, and you've taken him to the hospital a dozen times in the middle of the night lately. This is John Hasselstrom, his brother, south on highway 79." Over my shoulder, I saw Mother turn the thermostat down to fifty degrees. Then she came into the kitchen winding her alarm clock.

"What are you doing?" Her voice rose as she reached for the phone. "You can't do that!" As I hung up, she grabbed my shoulders, "I could just shake you when you disobey me, missy!" She raised her hand. I recoiled, remembering how she used to slap my face when I annoyed her. Gently, I put my hands on her shoulders, startled by their fragility, and held her at arm's length so she couldn't reach my face. I felt as if I might shatter her bones if I pushed too hard. "Get dressed, Mother. We'll follow the ambulance in."

She jerked back and ran into the dining room, wailing, "She hit me! My daughter hit me!"

I knelt beside my father to tell him an ambulance was coming. Eyes closed, he swung his arm, knocking my glasses off with the back of his hand. "I'll show you whether I'm boss in my own house or not," he said coughing.

Afraid the ambulance would miss our road in the dark, I drove to the highway, recalling how a local family ended up in jail in a similar situation. When his father died, the young rancher took over the family place, married, and moved his wife into a trailer so his mother could continue to live in her own house. Fiercely independent, the old lady supervised every detail of ranch work. One evening, when the young couple visited her—the wife usually washed dishes while the husband talked—they found her lying on the floor. She'd stay in her own house, the woman insisted, because if she went to a hospital, someone would put her in a nursing home. If they called a doctor, she'd rewrite her will, leaving the ranch to a daughter. The young people put the woman to bed. For several days, they fed and cared for her. When she grew weaker, they finally called a doctor. In the hospital, doctors discovered that her hip was broken, and she eventually died. A few days later the couple was arrested—handcuffed in the middle of their day's work—and jailed for murder. They were exonerated only after a long trial and considerable community chaos.

Behind me, I saw the dining room and bedroom lights go out. Ten minutes later, I flashed my headlights at the sheriff's car, and it followed me down our road with an ambulance trailing behind. By the time I parked by the garage, the ambulance had backed into the driveway and the sheriff was knocking on the back door. "Sorry we're a little late," he said. "Went to Harold's first. Kind of a habit, I guess."

I unlocked the door and led him inside, switching on lights as the dining room filled with tall, red-faced men.

"Hello, Sheriff," my father said, opening his eyes. "Haven't seen you in a while." He glanced around as a young man dropped a medical bag and another knelt beside him. "How are you fellas tonight?"

"We're pretty good, John. Question is, how are you?" said the sheriff. One man timed my father's pulse while another, frowning, spoke into a portable telephone.

My mother appeared in the bedroom doorway, rubbing her eyes and mumbling, "What in the world's going on?"

"Tell me, Sheriff—Drummond, is that your name?" my father said, "What do you think of kids that try to tell their parents what to do? My daughter here wants to put me in a hospital or a nursing home so she can steal my ranch." The sheriff frowned at me, and two of the men glanced up.

"Look in the bathroom," I said. "I'll be outside."

I sat on the back steps, mind blank, until the sheriff came out to say the ambulance was ready to leave. "You'd better help your mother get dressed," he said quietly. "She seems a little confused, but she'll want to be there." The EMTs strapped my father on a litter while I helped Mother button her jacket and lifted her into the front seat of my Bronco. Buckling both seat belts, I nudged my pistol farther under the driver's seat, afraid she'd see it and have hysterics. She was busy telling me how embarrassed she was that I called the ambulance. "Everyone will know, and it's all for nothing! You'll have to pay for the ambulance bill, young lady. And tomorrow I'm going to that hospital and get your father out, and then we'll make an appointment at the Mayo Clinic for later in the summer." Her face flashed red every few seconds, reflecting the lights of the ambulance ahead of us before it disappeared into darkness. "And once we get a date at Mayo's," she said, "you'll have to move home or my plants and my cats will die and it will be your fault."

The ambulance swung onto the highway and moved away, accelerating fast. Speedometer needle on seventy, I kept pace, staying far enough back so my headlights wouldn't distract the other driver. The dark settled down over both vehicles, and our lights made puny holes in the vast black plains.

Looking for the Dark: Buffalo Winter

Walking Frodo around a lake in a Cheyenne park on summer evenings, I often watched ducklings learning to swim, recalling the summer my neighbor Margaret raised some. Her husband, Bill, had mowed into a duck's nest while haying. He stopped the tractor at once and looked for the hen's body, assuming he'd killed her while she huddled protectively on the nest. He didn't find it, but he reasoned that even if the hen was alive, she might be hurt and might never return to her eggs. So he tucked them gently into his hat and took them home to Margaret, who slipped them under a setting hen until a dozen ducklings hatched.

She built a shallow pond in the backyard, where the ducklings learned to swim while their foster mother clucked nervously beside it. Margaret whistled to call her chickens to a daily ration of grain, but the flock, including the little duck family, also foraged in the yard and fields. Once she heard the hen cackling in alarm and saw the little ducks swimming on a nearby stock dam. As fall approached, the ducklings began watching migrating flocks, and one crisp day Margaret called to tell me she'd watched them fly up, circling until they caught a strong south wind. "Like kids," she said, "they have to leave. I suppose once Bonnie goes off to college, she won't really come back." The next spring, when she saw a dozen ducks fly over the house in tight formation, she whistled.

They circled low, quacking, and settled on a dam in the pasture, but none of them came near the house.

Go play with the towns you have built of blocks,
The towns where you would have bound me!
I sleep in my earth like a tired fox,
And my buffalo have found me.

—Stephen Vincent Benet
A Ballad of William Sycamore

Back in Cheyenne I am still angry at my parents' refusal to realize the seriousness of their situation. The morning after my father's dramatic collapse, I drove my mother to the hospital and left her visiting with Father while I hunted up the attending physician. Too busy to talk to me in his office, he paused in a hallway, holding his clipboard between us. I explained that both my father and my mother had given him incorrect information the night before and suggested he get their medical records from the Mayo Clinic.

"Since I'm treating him for an ulcer, I'm not sure that's relevant," he said, glancing at his watch. "If he follows the diet I'm ordering for him, he should have no further trouble."

Exactly the problem, I told him—because both of them are forgetful, he can't or won't follow directions. I begged the doctor to keep my father hospitalized for a few days and asked him to help me arrange an appointment with a heart specialist and someone who could analyze my father's mental state.

The young doctor looked over his narrow glasses at me. "I'm in internal medicine," he said. "That's all I can treat." He spun and walked down the hall. I spent all afternoon calling doctors in Rapid City, trying to get someone to examine my father more fully, with no success. The Mayo Clinic would not release copies of his records to the hospital without my father's authorization. The next morning, by the time I'd fed the cattle and got to my parents' house, my mother had already driven to the hospital. My father had been released.

"I'll show you what happens when you try to stick me in a hospital so you can steal my ranch," he said. As my father drove home at forty miles an hour, I followed, fuming. It's not the job of a specialist in internal medicine to consider how a patient weakened from loss of blood and a hospital stay might drive on a dangerous highway.

Too upset to write, I sort photographs moved to Cheyenne from my ranch house. Staring at a picture from my first wedding, I feel I am looking at two strangers. The bride's face is bland above her long dress of ivory velvet; the freckled groom is smiling. I made the dress myself, and in the picture I held a single rose so that my ruby engagement ring would show. I slumped a little, already diminishing myself to match Daniel. Several years after this picture, we returned to the ranch in an attempt to repair our marriage.

Why, I wonder, could I face the possibility of living on the ranch with my parents then but find it so repugnant now? Stupid question. I'm two decades older, and my determination to write has grown stronger every year. When I left the ranch for college, I should have, like the ducks, circled once or twice and kept right on flying. Even at thirty, when I believed my chances for love had been ruined by a bad marriage, I should have found courage enough to try life elsewhere. Approaching fifty, I have found, loved, and lost a better man than Daniel ever was, and have more confidence in the infinite variety of love.

My second husband, George, agreed with me that our marriage was improved by all that we had each learned in our first union. We became friends, growing into comfortable silences before we married. We learned patience by taking one breath at a time. We made mistakes and forgave each other, learning how to appreciate our time together. Now if I am to stay in Cheyenne with Jerry, I owe him the same attention. I've made my parents my first priority, but it's time to give up.

The photograph has sent me slipping out of control, back into memories of my relationship with Daniel. When we met, I was doing post-graduate study at the University of South Dakota, working nights for a daily newspaper. Daniel was seven years older and divorced, with three children. At age twenty-three, I'd sampled the sixties' smorgasbord of possibilities, supported myself, and knew how to live happily alone. I was ready for something different, so in 1966, Dan and I married and moved to Columbia, Missouri. There, he studied philosophy while I took graduate courses in literature and taught journalism at a women's college. Working two jobs and going to school, I tested my father's belief that persistence and hard work could solve any problem. When a professor told me I wasn't smart enough for graduate school, I took another of his Henry James seminars to prove him wrong.

After I discovered Dan's infidelities, I kept believing my marriage would be perfect if I only worked a little harder. But my trust in him eroded more each time he had another affair, and I began to distrust the academic world too. Midway through my second seminar on the novels of Henry James, I realized I'd rather fix fence than read another monotonous line. The next time I caught Daniel with another woman, I raged and broke things, scaring him pure long enough for us to return to South Dakota together. We thought a year away from the city might bring us closer. Longing for a permanent home, I pictured myself working with my father until I inherited the ranch. We built a fifteen-by-twenty apartment at the side of my parents' house, a quick and practical shelter while we made decisions.

While Daniel worked at his novel we started a literary magazine, and I cooked, cleaned, chopped wood, and helped my father with daily ranch work. Despite our frugality, Daniel was unable to make support payments for his children. I no longer remember why his problem required me to teach at a college eighty miles away, but we rented an apartment in that small town, and I drove back to the ranch each weekend to help my father.

Then Daniel got a traveling job as an artist in schools with the South Dakota Arts Council, bought a yellow Volvo, and started getting phone calls from women with whispery voices. Looking for a map one day, I found a pair of black lace panties in the glove compartment. Mine were white cotton.

I filed for divorce, but I'd signed a teaching contract and had to finish out the academic year. Daniel took our dog and most of the antique furniture I'd refinished and moved to Montana, leaving me the arts magazine and thousands of dollars in unpaid printing bills. In January, a neighbor in my apartment building introduced me to a towering Air Force veteran with long hair, George Randolph Snell. He was so handsome that I didn't trust him, but I fell in love anyway.

Still, afraid of marrying again so soon, I retreated to the ranch apartment. Editing the magazine, I realized I hadn't written anything for the seven years of my marriage and slowly began recapturing the skill and desire to do so.

My divorce from Dan was finalized in July just before my thirtieth birthday. I celebrated with George but fled back to the ranch at dawn with no intention of ever leaving it again. I could make a modest living, keep body and mind healthy by teaching as well as ranching, I thought, planning never to remarry.

I become easily lost in the details of that cold Dakota winter even though I am in Cheyenne, my study window open to the summer heat and street noises. I've always thought of the season after my divorce as the winter of the buffalo, because spending a few hours with the bison herd in Custer State Park one night changed me forever. When I left the great beasts, I had already turned my back on people like Daniel. Bold as any buffalo, I walked into my future.

I'd just found my first gray hair when a blizzard hit that November. In western South Dakota, winter strikes suddenly. One day everyone drives into the Black Hills to look at the vividly colored trees. The next, snow whirls the leaves into piles and drifts them under. City newspapers publish pictures of buffalo, calm and warm in the storm's eye.

Often, the first nasty blizzard is followed by warm days until weather prophets whine about a brown Christmas. Sunny days with temperatures in the seventies may occur until early January but the cold and snow always return. Gray days of sleet rule February. Our deep snowfalls come in March, April, even May, the months when ranchers' herds are calving. On January 22 of 1943—the same year I was born in Texas—Spearfish, a northern Black Hills town, saw the temperature rise forty-nine degrees in two minutes, setting a world record for swift temperature change. The only consistent plains weather pattern is variety.

For two months, the snowdrifts climbed fences while temperatures dropped. In late December, flakes stopped tumbling from the sky and froze solid on the ground. The thermometer hung at thirty degrees below zero through New Year's Eve. The first ten days of January brought a Chinook, and with tropical air swirling around us, my thermometer rose to fifty degrees. Piles of snow I considered permanent crumpled and gurgled down the draws.

One night, I put my feet on the hearth as usual and start reading. But I can't relax. By midnight I've already gone through my usual ritual of sleeplessness: pacing the floors, reading a chapter in one book, a page in another, washing dishes. I've dusted useless wedding presents I moved a dozen times during our marriage. In spite of being sick of ice, I pour gin over some and step outside with my drink to look at stars and listen to a great horned owl. The liquor sets my nerves on edge, quickens my pulse.

Suddenly I realize I don't have to stay in the cramped apartment. The warm spell cleared snow from most roads, and by a shortcut I can be in the Black Hills in a half hour. In the house, I keep seeing mud I should wash away. But driving will help relax me. The winding trails will be deserted and challenging. If the booze has made me dangerous, I won't hurt anyone but myself.

I step outside into floodlights: a swollen moon is rising, dull gold. The pickup starts at once. The thermometer reads twenty degrees. The air no longer hangs in the chilly paralysis of the past month and a half but feels gently warm. No other car moves on the highway. Once I turn onto the dirt road—a back way I use to evade the state park tollbooths—I push the headlight button in and drive by moonlight. Slowly. Savoring.

Houses and barns are murky blocks. When I lift my foot from the accelerator, the pickup drifts quietly, unseen, past my sleeping neighbors. The moon catapults blue-black tree shadows across the road, so thick and dark I expect a bump when the pickup noses into them.

On a back road into the state park, I watch for reflected light from animals' eyes, more subtle by moonlight than by headlight. Pink flashes mark deer raising their heads. Apparently, a pickup without lights is no threat, and they graze again. The pickup eases up a slope with little pressure on the gas pedal, idling to a stop as I see humped shapes, the hill in miniature. Rocks. No.

Buffalo.

I brake tenderly and turn off the ignition key. When the door opens, the dome light makes me squint. I close the door quietly and climb up the road bank through hissing buffalo grass. Sinking down, I fold my legs and sit with my back straight. I inhale deeply.

Blue moonlight reflects off an eye that looks as big as a dinner plate, flickers on a black horn as a head turns. Another. Like soldiers awaiting a dawn attack, they lie with mute sword blades unsheathed. My eyes adjust. Acres of curled hair lie like a plateau before me.

The pointed horns are everywhere, glittering in the moonlight, aiming at the sky. I imagine my ears opening like flowers, becoming more sensitive. Grass mutters. I hear a coyote in the Badlands, an owl glide out of the tree beside my prairie house. The breath of fifty bison, a hundred, inhaling my scent makes the ground shake, trees quiver. I feel I am inside earth's lungs.

Alarmed or angry buffalo make a huffing sound, blowing air from their nostrils in quick bursts. When a horse does it, we say "he has rollers in his nose" and settle into the saddle because we know he will buck. The herd is making its collective decision about me as I grasp my danger.

Briefly, I consider my position. I sit two pickup lengths, perhaps four strides, from the nearest cow. Dozens of other buffalo lie beyond her. Easily annoyed and unpredictable, bison can run faster than a horse and spin with the speed and agility of a dancer even though they may weigh a ton.

Buffalo are fickle. Even those raised in captivity have gored their owners to death. Angry bison demolish cars, tumbling them like a child's ball. Sharp-edged hooves chop and dice anything a stampeding herd runs over. I once saw a bull toss his head like a high school girl flipping hair out of her eyes. He disemboweled the bull beside him with one motion.

Now, in early January, the cows must be heavy with the weight of calves. Are buffalo irritable during pregnancy?

No matter. I'm not fast enough to untangle my legs and get inside the pickup before a buffalo is upon me. Since they can sense fear, I relax, breathing in the warm air rising from the hulking forms, buffalo musk. Try not to think how the hide hunters shot until the gun barrels were too hot to touch, took only tongues or hides. Left rotting carcasses so thick on the plains men said they could walk from Texas to Canada without stepping on the ground. Remnants of the herds were saved in a roundup directed by a descendant of French trappers and the Lakota natives of the prairie, the people to whom these Black Hills were sacred. When the herds grew, some were penned where tourists could drive among them. "Buffalo are dangerous. Stay in your cars," say the signs, but the animals look massively slow, plodding along dusty trails to water. Every year a few tourists get too close, die from goring or being crushed by hooves or head.

On this winter hillside, tranquility flows like a current from the massed bodies before me. I am soothed and I begin to feel serene. An almost imperceptible change draws my attention to the herd again. Soundlessly, the bulls materialize, moving out. Standing two long steps away, they form a massive curtain of lowered heads and moonlit eyes level with mine. The curved horns all point my way. Bronze statues, real buffalo. My hands rise from my lap, palm up, open, in a gesture so old and instinctive I am unaware of moving: *Peace. I have nothing to hide.*

Murmuring mixes with grumbles and rhythmic panting, like a distant crowd beginning to grow impatient. In a corner of my brain, a screen lights to show me how I may look if they all advance upon me. I switch it off.

After a while, I inhale deeply, starving for oxygen. The buffalo seem to vibrate. Air shifts gently against my face. One by one, the great bulls lie down with soft grunts and sighs. Joints creak as they fold their legs, still screening the cows and calves with their bodies. Shelter and fellowship made substantial. *Unh unh unh,* they grunt in an eternal, reassuring undertone.

Time swirls, or perhaps I fall into a trance, hallucinate. Some might say I am influenced by the alcohol ingested three hours ago. Or perhaps my fear of the buffalo heightens my perceptions. Samuel Johnson remarked, "Depend upon it, sir, when a man knows he is to be hanged in a fortnight, it concentrates his mind wonderfully." I think facing the buffalo is my soberest moment ever. My body remains in place, but I am not aware of it or of anything earthly for a long time.

Eventually, I notice the moon settling into the spiky trees. My legs are numb. The bulls still lie quiet. Some sleep, heads lowered. I lean on one haunch, get the opposite foot flat on the ground, and force myself up, locking my knees. Blood surges through my veins. I turn my back on the bulls and walk back to the truck. Several heavy heads turn when the engine catches and the truck begins creeping along the road. A hundred yards away, I shut the door firmly. The sound, loud as a gunshot, startles me sane.

In a hushed dream of moonbeams and buffalo bulls I drive down the dirt road until the pickup slides into a snow bank on a curve. My faithful truck wiggles playfully along the frozen track while I fight the wheel, and shimmies into the ruts like a nightclub stripper. Then it dives to the side—leaving the stage at intermission—finished with the set, smile gone.

By reflex, I gun the engine, trusting weight and momentum to carry the truck through. But I feel the truth in my buttocks and hands; I am stuck. I try to picture the pickup's box. Did I put the shovel back after the last time I dug myself out of a drift in the pasture?

When I step out of the truck, I leave the engine running, heater on. The buffalo are less than a half mile behind me, but the night has changed. Gnarled trees menace. The track ahead lies buried for thirty feet in hard-crusted snow. Under the truck, the pickup's gear box and springs are jammed with ice. To drive ahead means pushing a growing drift. The shovel lies across two bales of hay and six sacks of cattle cake I loaded in November for weight.

Behind the truck, my tracks run straight. Thinking I might be able to back out, I get in the seat, straighten the wheels, and shift into reverse. The pickup moves an inch before the tires begin to whir, whining in falsetto.

When I hear that moan for more than two minutes, I sneer at a driver who's angry, stupid, or both. The truck isn't going anywhere. Instead, the snow beneath will turn to ice from the friction as the tires rotate in vain. Miles of future travel will disappear into the air as the tires' tread wears away. An old man I knew drove into his pasture one winter day to check his cattle. When he got stuck, he spun the tires until they burst into flames. He burned to death in his truck. The family will never know exactly what, if anything, he was thinking.

I shut off the engine and get the shovel. Without haste, I dig straight, smooth tracks behind the rear tires to the spot where I drove into the drift. My numb hands grow clumsier as I work. I feel like curling up to sleep in the road. The night seems colder and throbs with strange noises. Once I think I hear a car motor idling nearby and look hopefully up the road for headlights. Then I return to digging. I am a woman alone on a back road, unarmed, at three in the morning. No time to be hoping for passers by.

Once I've shoveled a broad track nearly to bare ground, I get back in the truck, whimpering with cold, and hold my hands to the heater vents until my fingers will bend. Then I shift gently into reverse, applying a light kiss of accelerator. The engine murmurs, grows louder. I am sweating, trying to sense the angle of all four wheels, to keep them straight in the track. I feel the moment the gearbox begins dragging snow. Then the truck lurches sideways and settles again.

All four tires have slithered out of the track, deeper into the snow between the frozen road surface and the bank. I begin digging a new set of tracks beside the first.

I alternate digging with careful backing for two hours. My watch reads five A.M. when I finally back free of the drift. My eyeballs feel gritty. The shining images of buffalo stand in a small blue space far away. The shovel clangs as it strikes the tailgate. I turn the heater on high and drive wide around the drift, staying in the center of the road and away from the treacherous ditches.

I haven't gone fifty feet when headlights appear in my rearview mirror, nearly startling me into another drift. I have crossed no other tire tracks. What is anyone doing in the buffalo pasture at this hour?

The thought makes me laugh aloud, a demented sound after my silent night. But it is strange, in this neighborly country, if someone knew I was stuck and didn't offer help.

I head for the main road instead of the shortcut. The other pickup catches up with me as I drive down a hill to the highway. When I stop, it rolls up nearly to my bumper, headlights catching me like a spotlight. I am tempted to get out, confront him, but the kind of fear women feel most intensely on lonely roads at night stops me. I lock my door and drive on. The county seat town is the other way. In my direction lies nothing but dark ranch homes for thirty miles. Stiff with tension, I drive precisely at the speed limit until the road forks again and I head toward home. If he is a forest official, or someone going to work early, or even a poacher, surely he will be glad to turn, to be rid of me.

He follows. No matter what speed I drive. I pull to the shoulder through straight stretches, enticing him to pass, but the glaring lights remain five feet from my bumper. I begin to consider and discard wild schemes for evasion. Alone in my truck, I explain to the other driver about my sleeplessness, my drive, how I got stuck. I urge him to develop urgent business somewhere else.

Then I remember the motor I heard. Perhaps he parked out of sight near me for two hours. On a curve, I lean out my window and look back. Yes—I see a Forest Service insignia on the truck door.

By the time I reach the highway junction, I've answered my own questions. He lives in one of the cabins maintained for the men who regularly work with the buffalo herd. Perhaps he, too, was unable to sleep. When he heard my pickup, he investigated. I was driving with my lights off—cause for suspicion. Why would he think anyone drove by moonlight for entertainment? Had he known I was a woman, he might have helped me, but he couldn't find out who I was without approaching. Unidentified people might be armed and nervous poachers. The government doesn't pay him to help idiots who get themselves stuck in the middle of the night.

So he waited, sitting comfortable and warm, perhaps listening to the radio, until he saw my truck's license plates, saw the truck bed didn't contain a deer or buffalo carcass. No doubt he scribbled my license number and description on a note pad. I cooperated by sticking my head out the window. Blond female, orange Ford pickup, licensed in the same county. If he has a CB radio and has called the sheriff's dispatcher, he might already know who I am. In this county, he probably knows the date of my divorce and how much I weigh.

When I turn south on the highway leading to the ranch, the other pickup turns around and goes back toward the park. Relieved, I concentrate on getting home, thinking of the rumors if I meet any of my neighbors on the highway.

"Saw that Hasselstrom girl coming home at sunrise. She must be leading a wild life in town since she got divorced." No one would believe the truth even if I told it.

The yard is utterly black as I put the pickup away at six-thirty. Sunrise is an hour away. As I open the door of the apartment, cold air smelling of dead ashes sweeps out of the fireplace and engulfs me, as if all my worries have waited in this room for me to return. I face another day of pitching hay to cows, three more months of winter before I am likely to see green grass. Divorced in a neighborhood where folks marry for life, I may live like this until I die, with no more company than an independent cat. The thought no longer frightens me.

I flip the switch on a stove burner, put the teakettle on, and put fresh coffee in the drip pot. I arrange wood in the fireplace, then study the brass sculpture of a buffalo on the mantel. A one-dimensional figure carved from a slice of bronze, it is nothing like the winter buffalo in the hills or in my skull. Daniel and I knew the artist, a notorious womanizer who died a few years ago of Hodgkin's disease.

Right after our divorce, Daniel wrote to ask for the statue, saying he packed in such a hurry he forgot it. Funny, he remembered to take the antique icebox I refinished. Sipping fresh coffee, I box the sculpture and address it to him. I have no more reason to keep it.

After a hot shower, I sleep, dreaming of buffalo bulls with gleaming horns, a glowing language that is not words. Sitting before the bison herd, I sensed a holiness I didn't understand. Because I waited patiently, opened my mind, I learned something important from the vigilant herd's silence. Living on the plains for ages, bison have forged deep connections to the grasslands, while humans have survived only briefly on the prairie's surface, doing so much damage in our tenure. From some past reading, I recall a Zen-like line: "Before enlightenment, haul water, chop wood. After enlightenment, haul water, chop wood."

In the presence of the buffalo, I began to understand how I might deepen my own partnership with the plains. Driving dark highways alone or walking down city streets, I often breathe moonlight and remember.

Beekeeper

As our love deepened, Jerry and I decided to begin our life as a couple
symbolically, in a home that hadn't previously belonged to either of
us. We used savings to buy another house in Cheyenne, splitting the
cost equally.

Moving in, we were immediately conscious of how many other
people had occupied it before us. We swept and scrubbed their filth
from the woodwork and floors, peeled off wallpaper older than my
mother, and pulled up stinking carpets to lay new rugs over fir floors
hidden from sunlight for three generations. Working to correct inept
remodeling and dangerous repairs, we each said, warily, that it might
take us years to make the place our own. Together we began to weave
the separate and raveled threads of our lives into a new tapestry, a
skein of peace.

Still, I was often unable to sleep as the unfamiliar clamor and heat
of the city rose around me. I wandered through the house, as I walked
among the rocks and grasses around my hilltop house, trying to learn my
path as thoroughly. Hidden in darkness, I felt my way along the passages,
my fingertips memorizing peculiarities. The house was built about 1911,
soon after my father was born. In an architectural style called Prairie

Cube, its height and stark symmetry contrasted with my low prairie house and its wide views, making me realize how often I had lived in houses built by people I knew. In eighty years, the city house had housed boarders, been a coroner's home, and sheltered a family with eight foster children. Sometimes I thought I could hear those former tenants whispering behind me and wondered who would tiptoe up the stairs when I was dead.

Walking the dark hallways, my pupils widened to catch the glow of street lamps, and I sometimes scented sage smoke—perhaps it seeped from the trunks in the bedroom. I remembered how George and I worked together to build our Windbreak House. He dug its foundation into native limestone. Friends and neighbors helped us pour the basement and erect the frame. Our blood and sweat dried in the beams and floorboards of that house as we grew into a working team. Calluses told us where each two-by-four stood inside the walls, how each window fit its frame, how well our lives meshed. We exchanged sustenance with the surrounding prairie, body and spirit. Every fall, I borrowed George's pocket comb to harvest tiny grass and wildflower seeds, scattering them on the hillside. Grouse gathered to feed in the windbreak, sipping water from leaks in the waterlines I arranged to the native bushes and trees we'd planted. Just so, George and I began to fit ourselves into our little community around the ranch.

One of the pumps has been shot away, it is generally thought we
 are sinking.

—WALT WHITMAN

"Song of Myself"

Down, down, down into the darkness of the grave
Gently they go, the beautiful, the tender, the kind;
Quietly they go, the intelligent, the witty, the brave.
I know. But I do not approve. And I am not resigned.

—EDNA ST. VINCENT MILLAY

"Dirge without Music"

I barely noticed Margaret when we both rode the community
school bus to the larger town north of us; I must have been a high
school freshman when she entered first grade. The school bus
deposited us in her father's driveway, directly across the highway
from mine. Her older brother lunged out the door before it was
fully open and stalked up the hill, heavy work boots scattering
gravel, while Margaret scrambled behind him. I remember her
chestnut pigtails bobbing in rhythm with the pumping of her short
legs. After they went out of sight, a quarter mile away, I could still
hear him bellow, "Hurry up, Margaret Jean!"

Not long after I moved back to the ranch after divorcing Daniel,
I met Margaret's father and wasn't surprised when he remarked that
college was wasted time since I was back on the ranch, adding that if
I'd married a rancher, I'd have produced something more worth-
while than books by now—a couple of heirs.

Then George came into my life, a man whose first marriage had
ended the same winter as mine. Five years after meeting as teacher
and student, we wed and established our home.

We got acquainted with our closest neighbors—Margaret, her husband, Bill, and their daughter, Bonnie—in a natural way for a rural community. Their living room windows looked out on our pasture west of the highway. To use that pasture, we moved cattle through an underpass, a dark tunnel that made the cows nervous. Often, they either balked or ran through the fence onto the highway, where they'd dash back and forth among the trucks and cars. One day, working slowly and quietly, we eased a few cows and calves through the underpass and into the pasture.

The last cow in line spun on her back hooves and jumped the fence into the ditch beside the highway. Head high and eyes wild, she started trotting, looking back across the highway, perhaps thinking her calf was lost. I scrambled through the fence to head her off, hurrying because I could hear a semi climbing the other side of the hill. Roaring downhill, the truck would obliterate anything in its path.

Suddenly, a pickup stopped on the shoulder of the road, spraying gravel. Bill jumped out, yelling to turn the cow toward George, who opened the gate for her. Margaret ran and joined me, jogging along beside the cow and waving her away from the truck barreling past. While the cow located her calf and the bunch spread out to graze, we all leaned on the pickup to visit, shouting above the traffic noises.

Rushing to help in a crisis is normal rural behavior, but that conversation began our friendship with Margaret and Bill. They'd moved onto a rundown place on the dirt road she walked as a child, turning it into a tidy farm. They hauled truckloads of trash out of the dusty yard and tore down some of the rickety buildings, thriftily saving good boards to patch other sheds. They lived in a concrete-block basement until they could raise a house with south windows and a deck on the east so they could watch the sunrise and visitors approaching.

Margaret dug a huge garden and raised chickens, canning and freezing much of their food. She hauled pasture stones to terrace the yard and planted ferns and flowers. Each year she planted more trees on all four sides of the yard, creating windbreaks around their oasis.

Whenever Margaret and I talked, we discovered interests in common. We both read poetry and subscribed to magazines that informed us about the environment and the role of women in the world, topics that didn't interest most of our neighbors, including our mothers. Political leaders urged that our part of the state support a uranium mining industry and establish a nuclear waste dump for the nation nearby, so we joined the same environmental organization and traded driving to meetings in the city twenty miles away. Faces shadowed in the soft light of the dashboard dials, we spoke more freely about our lives than most women do in small communities.

Both of us lived next door to our parents. Our hard-working fathers were friends who taught us lessons we appreciated, but they also held views we disliked. Reading and going to meetings, they said, were just "wasting daylight." Going to town for any purpose except buying necessities—defined as tractor parts—proved young people couldn't do a full day's work.

I don't recall which of us brought up the subject, but one night we both started giggling about how her whole family went to town together. Her dad drove, with either her brother or her husband in the front passenger seat. Margaret, her mother, and her sister-in-law squeezed into the back like tomatoes in a carton. Her father mapped errands so they started on one side of town and ended up on the other, with no backtracking allowed. "He always says we don't have time if we women want to shop for clothes," she added.

"How can you stand it?" By that time, I was used to traveling alone, determining my own schedule.

"It's the only time I can talk to my mother or sister-in-law without my dad or my brother answering," said Margaret. Now I realize how often in our discussions Margaret would look at the topic in a way I'd never considered. No matter how completely I'd researched and considered an idea, she often voiced a viewpoint that had never occurred to me.

Soon we were having telephone conversations nearly every evening after supper, voices murmuring to the gentle tune of silverware clinking and the hiss of rinse water as we satisfied the work ethic and enjoyed ourselves. A mile apart, we might have been sisters sharing work and confidences at the same sink. Instead of talking about work or gossip, we talked about what we were reading, or about our roles as women in a state and community that still regarded females as subordinate. We acknowledged that our mothers had given up their freedom, but we disagreed about the solution. I argued that only passage of the Equal Rights Amendment would force society to acknowledge women's true equality. Margaret said that the ERA would create more problems than it solved. "Women are better off if they let men think they believe they are inferior," she said, "and then work undercover."

"Besides, if the job is shoveling grain out of the pickup," she added, "I can't shovel as long as Bill, so my labor isn't worth as much as his."

"But," I retorted, "if you hired a high school boy to help Bill shovel the grain, he'd expect more money than a girl for the same job," I said. "Yet they might shovel an equal amount."

"Linda, if you can find a woman today who can shovel as much as George—a big, *strong* woman," she giggled, "what will you do if she's pregnant in six months? She'll be more experienced, but she won't be able to lift as much. Will you cut her pay because she's not delivering equal work?" We could laugh about our debate, but we never agreed, just as we compromised with our fathers and mothers to keep peace.

Our discussions of women's issues naturally led to thoughts of children, and we learned what a certain telephone silence, a particular wobbly smile over a coffee cup meant. After having a daughter, Margaret was unable to have more children. Though I was happy in my second marriage, George was sterile from radiation treatments, so I'd never ride the plains with our children. I contented myself with my stepchildren and kept writing, while Margaret kept planting trees. "I want generations that will follow on this ranch to say, 'Those are the trees that Grandma and Grandpa planted way back in '72,'" she later wrote.

Recalling how our grandmothers made soap from scraps of fat after butchering beef and hogs, Margaret invited several women to make soap in her kitchen. She provided lye, practical experience, and the fat she'd rendered from the year's butchering. According to our preferences, we novices added ingredients, including sand to make hand soap and honey for bath soap.

That night, soaking in a hot bath with my personal chamomile soap, I realized that Margaret was living my fantasies, creating the life I'd imagined as a child. Merging her roles as wife and mother, she also acted as a responsible rancher and beekeeper, even when she disagreed with the majority. She never hesitated to challenge stereotypes but could explain her reasoning without fury.

Once I told Margaret about my argument with a lean vegetarian who contended I should set my cows free and grow vegetables. "I'm sick of environmentalists who buy veggies trucked in from California and say ranchers are wrecking the country," she said. "If they don't know why that's worse, my life isn't long enough to tell them. I can accomplish more by growing trees."

I often spoke at public meetings, but eventually decided I could use my writing skills to best educate readers about the environment. When my district representative actually poked me in the chest while telling me I should stay home and have babies, I raved to Margaret, "I'm tired of talking to men like that. No wonder people pour syrup in bulldozer engines." On my birthday a month later, I found an antique wrench on my front porch. I'd lent Ed Abbey's *The Monkey Wrench Gang* to Margaret, and we'd agreed that the environmental movement needed humor, but I wasn't certain she'd left the wrench. Was she suggesting approval of property destruction in a good cause? Puzzled, I asked. She admitted it, giggling. "I hope you don't hang around with a *lot* of people who might give you a monkey wrench!"

Often, we both stayed up late on long winter evenings to read, exchanging books and quotations more often than recipes. When I whined about rejected poems, she quoted Robert Frost's comment that poets have to *seem* businesslike because their wares "are so much harder to get rid of." Margaret suggested the title of my first book of poems, the phrase 'caught by one wing,' adding, "A lot of people could identify with that idea—not just those of us who live near our parents."

I often complained to Margaret when a book review called me a "woman writer" or "woman rancher," as if those were special, and perhaps inferior, categories. "They never say, 'He's a male writer,' or a 'male rancher,'" I pointed out. "How would you like to be described?" She was silent a long time before saying, "Beekeeper."

"You'd like that better than being remembered as a wife and mother?"

"Being a beekeeper is more unusual," she said. Her allergy to bee venom was so severe a single sting might have killed her, she said, so, "It was hard learning to be calm while the bees crawled all over me. I had to work at being a beekeeper. Some people become mothers by accident."

I called Margaret the minute I learned that the Old English word *keep* originally meant "to seize, hold, or guard," adding, "So you are not only raising bees, you are a guardian, a bee champion, the Lady of the Bees!"

She loved the idea. "You know, I wish I could go back to school. I just don't have enough time in the day to learn all I want to know."

"Margaret," I broke in, "your time is too valuable to waste listening to some guy drone on about 'iambic dissonances.' You don't need a master's degree—you live in the real world. You know more practical, useful things than most people with doctorates will ever know."

"Linda. Stop. I mean I'd like to graduate from college." I was flabbergasted into silence as she laughed, "I don't very often leave you completely speechless!"

I sputtered, "I had no idea. I mean, you read and talk as well as any college-educated person."

"Well," she explained, "the first time I realized you thought I'd graduated from college, I thought you might think less of me if you knew. I didn't know you as well then."

On another occasion, I interrupted one of Margaret's lectures about bee behavior to say impatiently, "Trouble with bees is that hive mentality, the same reason I hate ants, churches, and political parties. When everybody acts together, it makes me nervous. Humans in a mob are more violent than individuals."

"That's your trouble," she retorted. "You're too damned independent. Sometimes humans need to work together, even if they don't like each other. It's called compromise—you ought to try it."

On a snowy Thanksgiving Day in 1983, Margaret and her family drove to town for dinner with relatives. Anticipating a blizzard, Bill drove the ranch pickup with four-wheel drive, normally used only in the pastures. The seat belts had slipped behind the seats among lost wrenches and bits of hay, and they didn't take the time to dig them out. Near the bottom of a hill, state highway 79 narrowed for a bridge with high concrete abutments. Margaret told me later, "Just as we came over that long hill before the bridge, I felt filled with love, so I leaned over and said, 'I love you guys.'"

As they approached the bridge, a pickup veered toward them. Bill swerved and braked, but the two trucks collided head on. Margaret and Bill both got out of the truck, but Bonnie was pinned with her knees against the dashboard, screaming and swearing. Margaret said later, "I've never heard Bill say some of those words, even when a cow kicked him!"

Paramedics arrived and put Bonnie on a stretcher, assuring Margaret that injured people display surprisingly profane vocabularies—they'd heard it all before. When they realized Margaret had been in the truck as well, they examined her, discovered her back was broken, and loaded her on a stretcher.

That night, neighbors kept the telephone wires hot exchanging facts and rumors. The elderly couple in the new pickup that hit Bill's were killed outright. Their daughter arrived a few minutes later. She explained to the Highway Patrol how her father had bought the pickup earlier that day. She had argued that he shouldn't be driving, especially not an unfamiliar vehicle. Enraged, he had ordered her mother into the pickup and roared away. She followed and saw the accident that killed her parents and permanently altered Margaret's family.

Doctors wired Bonnie's jaw shut to hold loose teeth and stitched up a long cut on her forehead. More serious were the breaks in her thighbones, which had to heal before they could be set. Margaret lay immobilized in the same hospital room. Each time I visited, I could hear their laughter far down the hall as they kept each other's spirits up. The room filled with so many flowers that they sent some to other patients. Margaret was surprised how many neighbors sent gifts, but I reminded her that she was the only woman in the community who ever beat my aunt Josephine in acts of kindness.

A Highway Patrolman told Margaret that if they had worn seat belts, they might have walked away with nothing but bruises. When Margaret recovered enough to think about the accident, she began lecturing friends to fasten their seat belts, and campaigning to get elderly drivers off the highways. We'd often discussed the driving habits of both sets of aging parents, but now our conversations lapsed into bickering.

"You've got to do something about your mother," Margaret would say. "I've been hearing about a big white car with an invisible driver. The other day I saw her drive down the wrong side of the median. All the oncoming cars had to drive into the ditch."

When I made half-hearted attempts to talk to my parents about their driving, my mother cried, and my father bellowed, "By God, you want to take my driver's license so you can put me in a nursing home and steal my ranch!"

That winter, between arguments about our parents' driving, Margaret and I talked about the practical experience she'd gained planting trees and keeping them alive in our arid country, information that contradicted tree experts. Later, I once told mutual friends in Margaret's presence that I'd suggested she write a book.

"Not so fast!" she countered. "Writing the book was my idea. You writers always have to change the story. Well," she went on as I gaped, "you did encourage me. You read the rough draft and told me it wasn't awful." For seventeen months, Margaret fought pain in her back and legs as she wrote at the computer that Bill bought her. "Our fathers are both wrong," she said once. "This is the hardest work I've ever done."

In February, we both ordered young trees to add to our windbreaks. Margaret usually planted hers first in tin cans; there they would spend a year growing in the shade, where she could pamper them and save every one. I put mine directly into the ground, reasoning that while the shock of transplant killed some, at fifty cents a tree planting them only once was worth a few losses. In February, Margaret said she'd ordered five hundred pine trees. "It's my promise to myself that my back will be stronger, so I can plant them myself," she explained.

One day in May, she invited me for coffee. Walking stiffly, she met me at my car and led me behind her house. In the shade under her clothesline stood five hundred pine trees in separate cans. "I wish I had a camera," she said, "so you could see the look on your face."

"Dammit, Margaret, this isn't funny. You were going to call me so I could help," I sputtered. "You're not supposed to lie to your friends."

She shook her head. "You *asked* me to call. I never said I would."

"Lying by omission counts."

"Don't just stand there," she said. "Shut up and help me pull weeds." Passing me a slice of her Kahlua pie later, she said, "It is such a pleasure to *work*, to use my body as it was meant to be used."

The pain and stiffness in her back continued. Nearly two years after the accident, in April of 1985, doctors partially fused her spine, leaving it weak but improved. "Now I have to save my energy for important things," she declared, "like spending time with my family." Determined not to become an invalid, she devised ways to clean house without bending. She hired high school boys to help with heavy lifting in the bee yards. When Bonnie came home from college that summer, Margaret brought her into the bee business, gradually making her responsible for hiring help. "I want her to know how to give orders, help her learn how much she can do," Margaret explained. When Bonnie fired a young man without consulting her parents, Margaret was pleased that she'd trusted her own judgment.

As Margaret's back improved, her strength continued to decline. She often felt weak and nauseated, but she didn't have the flu. Thinking she'd become allergic to strong coffee, she gave it up for tea. She experimented with vitamins, drugs, and healthy diets. She went to a Minnesota hospital several times for tests, with Bonnie driving when she grew too weak to go alone. In a hospital hobby shop, Margaret bought a Ukrainian egg-decorating kit and learned how to dip each egg repeatedly in colored dyes, applying wax to create designs. She was excited to discover artistic abilities she'd never had time to cultivate and found the intricate work relaxing. "Isn't this perfect?" she said. "I care for the chickens that feed us eggs. Then I create art from the eggs and give them away. It's another form of recycling! Everything in our lives should fit together this way—a circle, only it's egg-shaped."

As we grew closer, Margaret learned that I often suffered from migraines so severe I vomited. "You shouldn't be alone when you feel that badly," she said. "I could bring a book and just sit in your living room until you felt better." Rural people seldom call each other after ten P.M. unless we need help in a dire emergency, such as a prairie fire. Often in the next few months, unable to sleep, I stood on my deck looking at my neighbor's yard light. If I dialed Margaret's number, I knew she would sit up beside her sleeping husband and talk or listen according to my need. The knowledge was enough.

All during the first winter after George died, Margaret and I talked on the telephone often, debating possible causes for the fact that she felt worse every day. Was she allergic to some food? She tried eliminating different foods from her diet for a week at a time. Had she been overexposed to the chemicals we all use to kill lice on the cattle? We both recalled helping our fathers spray cows, drenched in the stuff. From our battle to keep nuclear waste out of South Dakota, I'd learned about underground radiation. I researched the levels in our area, thinking that perhaps she'd had too much. Margaret read about airborne poisons from home furnishings. A doctor suggested that she might be allergic to household dust, so she bought a vacuum so powerful it removed dust mites. Our mailboxes bulged as we swapped articles and books on every possibility we considered. Every morning Margaret's voice sounded wearier and weaker.

We often talked about visiting one another, but the winter storms kept blowing more snow into our roads and the effort of digging out once more was too great. With my parents in Texas, I shoveled snow and fed cattle alone all day. When I called Margaret while I did dishes in the evening, she was often asleep. For a month we didn't see each other. Then one bright day in early 1989, she called to invite herself to my house at mid-morning. "And I'll bring your honey," she said. We'd made a ritual of her usual autumn visit, always on some day when the sun was warm but the air cool. I usually stepped out on the deck as she climbed the steps carrying a bulging bag. We'd hug, our bodies nudging the hard mass between us. She'd set four gallon jars in a row on my scarred dining room table while I pulled a pan of scones out of the oven. "Here's your bonus for being a good girl," she'd say, pulling from her purse a plastic container of honeycomb.

Sitting together, we'd look out the east windows to yellow cottonwood trees surrounding my parents' house and the gray lattice of corrals. Sunlight would shine through bubbles drifting in each sweet gold vessel. One of us always remarked how much the swells of tawny prairie looked like mountain lions sunning. We'd put chunks of fresh comb on scones and lick beeswax and honey from our fingers as we talked about how our trees were growing, about my writing, about her daughter's latest fad.

I hurried to bake scones before Margaret arrived, thinking I'd tell her that instead of celebrating fall, we were rejoicing that we had survived another Dakota winter.

When I stepped out on the porch to greet her, I tried not to stare. Her face was white and thin, her auburn hair was short and bouncy with curl. Hugging her, my cheek against hers, I saw a woven edge and realized she was wearing a wig. When she set the heavy bag on the table, her arms looked thin. She struggled to lift the first jar, then gave up and let me take them all out of the bag. The honey inside was cloudy, crystallized over the winter.

"Have you been a good girl?" she said with a half smile, taking the honeycomb container out of her purse, and we both laughed a little nervously. I hurried to pour tea, and we each took a bite of a buttered scone with fresh honey before Margaret sat back in her chair. "How are you doing, really?" she asked.

Eating better, I told her, after my doctor threatened to hospitalize me for malnutrition. George had been dead seven months. I was beginning to write, so I was starting to survive.

She nodded, then reminded me how we'd both puzzled over her symptoms. After we'd exhausted all the possibilities either of us could imagine, she'd started reading about the HIV virus. "I remembered that they gave me blood transfusions when they operated on my back," she said. So she asked the doctors to give her the HIV test. They thought she was joking. They carefully explained—"in one-syllable words," she reported with a grin—why a Lutheran housewife from rural South Dakota fit none of the risk categories. Margaret insisted, explaining, "I've had a lot of experience in the last few years with doctors who thought they knew what was best for me."

She took a deep breath. "Linda, I wish this didn't have to be now, and I wish it didn't have to be you. I tested positive. I have the HIV virus."

I tried to keep my face rigid. Margaret's voice was steady, her thoughts organized. "I'm not going to tell anyone except my family and you," she said. "I need someone to talk to outside the family. It has to be you." She shrugged. We both knew why. I sat, mute and stupefied, as she smiled and patted my arm. "Don't worry. I'm going to live until they find a cure."

I don't remember what else we talked about before she hugged me as she left. Crying, I washed her coffee cup with bleach, even though I knew enough about AIDS to know better. Then I washed my face with cold water and called my friend Tom, an artist and a homosexual who volunteers with AIDS patients. "I have a friend who's tested positive," I said, not telling him who, "and I need to know everything."

During the following months, Margaret and I talked often about what might happen when local people learned of her illness, as we believed they eventually would. "I'm afraid to put my coffee cup down at church," she said. "What if, later, someone is afraid because they might have drunk from it? I'm afraid to hold their babies."

I blushed and assured her that she wasn't responsible for the fears of ignorant people. Over and over, we debated keeping her secret. One night she reminded me that although no one in the community especially liked the rich family who'd built a new house not far from us, everyone donated food and clothing when their house burned.

"That's different," I snapped. "A fire isn't contagious. Most people think AIDS only affects people they consider weird or evil. Remember the news story about the hemophiliac boys with AIDS? Somebody firebombed their house. If people will do that to children, I don't think you should take the chance."

Margaret studied HIV the way she examined everything, aided without knowing it by the materials Tom supplied. Anonymously, she wrote an article about AIDS prevention for a Lutheran women's magazine. But keeping her secret burdened her. "It's like holding on to a handful of feathers," she said. "Every time I turn around, another one is floating away. I don't have much energy, and I'm wasting it chasing feathers," she said. After reading a dozen sympathetic letters from the magazine's readers, she began to consider giving up the secrecy.

Since she'd never lied before, she wasn't good at evasion. Friends asking about her illness sensed deception. Some called me, puzzled. "I'll bet she has cancer," said one. "She doesn't want people to know because that's a death sentence, and she doesn't want sympathy." Telling myself that I was protecting Margaret, I invented mysterious viruses and consultations with doctors. Once when I stopped at Tom's house to pick up several articles about HIV research, he guessed the truth. I hadn't broken my pledge to Margaret, but I was relieved to be able to cry on his shoulder.

Then someone asked Bonnie, four hundred miles away at college, if her mother had AIDS. Margaret called me, furious. Had I told?

"Of course not," I said. "But I'm the only one outside your family who knows. Naturally, you suspect me first. But look at the fix I'm in. If I tell you which of your relatives I don't trust, you'll either be angry at me or be suspicious of someone in your family." Together, we considered other possibilities, and I admitted that Tom had guessed. Margaret, who didn't know him, slammed the phone down at once. All that day and the next I tried to write, but in her offended silence all I could think of was how to apologize and assure her that my friend wouldn't tell anyone.

Long after dark the next night, working in the basement, I heard a knock. I switched on the yard light and recognized

Margaret's car before unlocking the door. She stepped inside and handed me a booklet titled, "A Tale of Two Friends on Adjoining Farms: A Story Being Written by Margaret and Linda."

Lately, the story began, she'd associated my name with *Linde,* German for linden tree. "Deep roots," she wrote. "Solid trunk." She identified herself with the buffaloberry shrub, "giver of fruit but possessed of defending thorns." When she's not sure life is all it's cracked up to be, she wrote, "Linda helps her keep things in perspective."

On the last page she'd written how I, too, needed someone to talk to. Since George was dead, I'd chosen to tell a friend who understood the disease. I was forgiven, she wrote. When I finished reading, she pointed to the last page. "It's perforated," she said. "Tear it out." I obeyed, and she hugged me. "Now it never happened. Good night." After I stopped crying, I fished the torn page out of the wastebasket to keep with the story.

Then, as she said, she "opened her hand and let the feathers fly." First, she talked with her minister, then revealed the truth to her friends. My phone rang as neighbors shocked by the rumor called, hoping I'd deny it. Margaret had pledged me to confirm the truth and educate people about the disease. Perhaps our neighbors were supportive because they'd known her all her life, but no one drew away. She wrote a second article for her church magazine revealing her name. "You hugged me," she said. "I should have known you would. The love flows into me with radiant warmth." Her phone rang constantly, she said, with supportive calls. A few responses made her angry. "So, how long do you have to live?" asked a cousin.

"I don't know," snapped Margaret. "How long do you have?"

After we talked ourselves hoarse in one telephone call, she said softly, "You know, right after the accident, I asked them to test for HIV in the blood they gave to Bonnie. I thought of asking them to test the blood they gave me when my back was fused, but I told myself it didn't matter. It couldn't happen. It wasn't important."

We were both silent for a long time, thinking of our mothers and grandmothers, of other women who put their husbands' needs, even their families' whims, above their own welfare. I started to speak, but she said first, "It's a high price to pay for not valuing myself enough, isn't it?"

———————

I need no advice on growing trees in the leafy city of Cheyenne, but I keep Margaret's book *Growing Trees on the Great Plains* on my desk so I can open it and read her note, "Plant On! Love, Margaret." She called me several times to talk about the joy of promoting the book. Though South Dakota newspapers rarely pay much attention to writers, several reporters interviewed Margaret because she was willing to talk publicly about AIDS, becoming front-page news in South Dakota, where cases were rare. She warned the writers, "Call me a woman, a mother, a wife, a beekeeper, or a writer, but don't call me a victim." She was more interested in talking with the people who came to bookstores to hear her talk about trees. "I shake the hand of someone who buys my book," she said on the telephone, "and know they'll be planting trees for years with my help. I'll be there with them."

Both of us fell silent. My only photograph of Margaret stands on a shelf high in my study, a black-and-white view of her back as she walks away through her trees carrying a shovel.

Badger's Business

Early one June morning, I walked Frodo in a Cheyenne park. Tugging
on the leash, he ran ahead and pushed his nose into a hole, sniffing and
whining. Only his chubby hindquarters were visible as his carrot tail
whipped back and forth. Marks of long claws in the dirt told me only a
badger could have dug the hole.

Astonishing—the badger was bold enough to conduct business five
feet from an asphalt trail traveled by dozens of runners and bicyclists.
Perhaps the badger migrated from an area that became too busy as housing developments spread over the plains in every direction from the city.
Maybe, like an old rancher, the badger had retired and moved to town.
What does he eat? Park employees routinely poison ground squirrels, but
perhaps he got by on baby ducks, frogs, and squirrels.

I dragged Frodo away from the hole, laughing as I recalled a story
my muzzle-loading friend Terry had told in his slow drawl. He'd gone
with a shotgun-toting friend to hunt turkeys in the Black Hills. Mean-
dering through the trees unarmed, Terry spotted a badger hustling away
and chased it, yelling for his buddy. The badger started to dig, half his body
underground in seconds. Terry grabbed the stubby tail, yanked and threw
in one motion, hollering, "Shoot! Shoot!" He let the silence build before
concluding, "First time I ever saw a badger shot on the wing."

Every day, Frodo explored the hole in the park while I spotted more evidence of badgers: shallow holes dug near mouse colonies, resting places scraped under bushes. Maybe badgers are adapting to human occupation, as have coyotes and mountain lions.

I've never seen the park badger, but maybe I'm becoming citified, missing the sight simply because I don't expect it. As my eyes adjust to straight lines and asphalt, it may be harder to see the wild even when I'm in it. I haven't yet lost my prairie eyes, though, since I often see badger dens as I drive: above gullies that run water once every five years, in stream banks, in railroad rights-of-way.

After seeing the den for the first time, I left Frodo in our fenced yard and walked to the library a block away, where I found new information. Once a seven-year-old boy lost from his family's home in Manitoba lived contentedly for two weeks in a badger's hole, nibbling leftovers. He emerged unharmed. How did it feel to sleep curled against a badger's thick fur, to hear that voice murmur gently instead of hissing? I envied that child.

Thinking about the city badger, I recalled childhood encounters with his country cousins. Whenever I found a hen's nest hidden outside the chicken house, under a tree or in an old tire, I watched for the chicks to hatch. Several times, both nest and hen vanished, leaving only feathers and shattered shells. "Badger," said my father when I showed him the evidence.

I knew badgers were numerous in our area because fresh piles of dirt appeared beside big holes in the pastures daily, suggesting that dozens of the furry bulldozers roamed the darkness. So I questioned my rural neighbors, asking what they thought of the critters. First they'd denounce badgers for digging holes, then bluster about shooting any badger they saw.

"But have you ever seen one?" I persisted. Almost everyone said no, eventually.

On a trip back from the ranch earlier in the summer, I stopped outside Cheyenne to walk Frodo along a drainage ditch near a particularly ugly housing development. Screened by tall grass at the edge of a field where toddlers romped were craters large enough to swallow a child. Perhaps Badger digs temporary dens to wait for peaceful hunting at suppertime. Or maybe he wants to play. Naturalists have seen badgers turning somersaults and doing a shuffle dance resembling the twist, playing leapfrog and king of the mountain. Even though the badger has a reputation as an irascible hermit, a silent sentry living underground and patrolling in darkness, he can live unobserved on the fringes of our lives. A keen sense of smell warns a badger so well that he escapes us before we see him. Even determined naturalists have trouble sneaking close.

When I lived on the ranch, however, much of my work required walking or riding in our pastures, where I often saw badgers without realizing how rare the encounters were. Once on an afternoon walk soon after George died, I fell into a badger hole. My senses must have been in an extremely heightened state, because even now, many years later, I have no trouble recalling the details of what happened that day.

I think I could turn and live with animals, they are so placid and
self-contained. . . . They do not sweat and whine about their
condition.

—WALT WHITMAN
"Song of Myself"

The commonplace I sing . . .
The open air I sing, freedom, toleration,
(Take here the mainest lesson—less from books—less from
the schools,)
The common day and night—the common earth and waters. . . .

—WALT WHITMAN
"The Commonplace"

Perched on a limestone outcropping in a neighbor's pasture two
miles west of my ranch house, I watch the sun drift behind the
Black Hills, remembering George's reminder with his last breath:
"Watch the sunsets!" The sun's fire dwindles to a peach glow, the
last warmth brushing my cheek. Sighing with me, the prairie settles
into darkness as I rise and step off the rock. Light seems to flicker
from the tips of tall grasses, but I walk waist-deep in black ink. I
hurry because my parents call each evening at dark to be sure I am
safe inside the house, locked away from the dangers of the world.

The contoured ridges near Windbreak House are so familiar I
can walk with my eyes shut, but tonight I'm walking on a neighbor's
land, where I've spent less time. In the dregs of daylight, I widen my
eyes to enhance my peripheral vision. Every object seems to reflect
the stars. To keep stickers out of my shirtsleeves, I hold my hands
outstretched, brushing the heads of grasses.

Then my right foot falls on air instead of earth. I plunge forward. My elbows smack into the dirt. I hang suspended, my left leg

doubled up to my hip and my right dangling in empty space. For an instant I can picture my broken body lying at the bottom of a dark shaft, an uncovered well, perhaps. I can picture skidding down a tunnel while I claw at dirt walls. Buried alive.

I push against the ground until I can sit on the hole's edge, rubbing bruises and scrapes, peering down in the ebbing light. Nearly four feet below, the bottom of the shaft is as wide as the top. On two sides gape small dark openings, maybe the original burrow of a ground squirrel the badger was hunting when he created this pit.

I stand up, warily testing my legs. Three more craters lie in an arc ahead. Limping a little after my tumble, I edge around the patchwork of holes, anxiously testing each step before committing my full weight. Maybe while I sat on the limestone outcropping to watch the sunset, a badger was prowling here, and he hid at the sound of my footsteps. In the dying light, I head for my house with my head turning from side to side, scanning the ground ahead for more holes, hoping to see the digger.

I see holes but no badger. His shaggy coat, fluctuating from gray to mottled brown with a yellow undertone, is perfect camouflage for a prairie evening. Straining my eyes, I look especially for the white stripe that marks Badger's neck from his collar to the tip of his short, pointed nose. His piratical black cheek patches are invisible in the shadows. When I stumble over a rock and throw my hands up to catch myself, I grab barbed wire and know I've reached the fence dividing our pasture and the neighbor's. Somewhere nearby, the badger prowls.

Unlike skunks and raccoons, badgers don't panhandle from humans or invade the storage sheds where ranchers and farmers store feed for domestic animals. A hungry badger will eat anything that doesn't eat it first, but they rarely come close enough to humans to kill pet cats or dogs.

Climbing between the barbed wires, I walk past the tall cedars in front of my parents' house, glad to stop looking at my feet. Through the lighted window, I see them sitting at the round oak dining room table, watching the early news. In a few minutes they will make their evening call.

Walking up the last long slope to my house, I can barely see the outline of my windbreak trees. The snow fences built out of railroad ties loom like a fortress against the stars. On my left stands the black mass of the ridge where I once met the king badger of that particular hill.

My house overlooks a dam that has been dry most of the sixty years since my uncle built it. Heavy spring rains turned it into a lake, bringing birds new to me: herons, snipes, and several species of ducks. Now I eat breakfast on the deck while watching birds through binoculars.

One Sunday morning, I resolved to walk around the lake, trying to see the common snipe, since I hear its winnowing call each night. Then I began climbing the ridge to photograph my home and the ephemeral lake from above. We always save the ridge pasture for cattle we need to keep close to the corrals. Since it's too rough to cover with a pickup, I often ride a horse to collect the cows. Several times, I had glimpsed quick movement at the mouth of a den or seen fresh tracks, but I'd never seen a badger on the ridge.

Ordinary prairie sights fill my climb. Redwing blackbirds dive past my head, safeguarding teacup-sized nests hung on brome grass. Nearby, a nest lies on the ground, pale green eggshells broken and licked clean as only a badger or raccoon will do. Frodo splashes in the lake, water plants dangling from his ears, sending killdeer skipping away on brittle legs.

High on the slope I see what my father calls a fairy ring, a circle of mushrooms rising above grass that is greener than usual. The circle is strewn with broken brown stems and caps where cattle, deer, and smaller nibblers like mice have dined. Yucca blooms burst white, regal on stiff stalks, swaying in the breeze blowing down off the hill. Then I step around a rock outcropping to check a bare patch of ground visible from my deck, and pause, expecting to see spider silk webbing the entrance of an abandoned fox or coyote den.

Instead, my gaze meets the wise, calm eyes of a badger. As I stare, he flattens himself against the ground, opening his mouth and inhaling until he looms large as a bear.

Frodo's tags jingle. In Scotland, Westies—bred with short legs and strong jaws and necks—are sent into badger dens to drive or drag the badgers out. Any dog meant to fight badgers needs perseverance, so I suspect Frodo's broad stubborn streak is part of the breeding plan. He's attacked pit bulls and malamutes without hesitation and survived, but I fear ancestral memory will kill him if he jumps the badger. I turn and snatch him up.

When I look again, the badger is gone. I scan the hillside. Near where the badger had been standing, a faint track in the clay points toward a small hole I hadn't noticed. The opening looks too narrow for the wide body; a badger's fur must make it slick as a watermelon seed. Though a den entrance is often littered with broken bones and rattlesnake rattles, the level shelf before this hole is clear of weeds and stones. An old badger, wise enough to be tidy.

How can a big, meat-eating predator remain so obscure among people who observe the prairie every day? How can we fail to see what is before our eyes?

I've learned that some badgers live communally in a main dwelling hundreds of years old, extending sixty feet into a hillside. Each badger in the clan may occupy a separate apartment, but they cooperate in hunt and play, and in raising a single litter of cubs each year. They don't hibernate but doze during cold weather, surviving on fat reserves between hunts. On nice days, they wake to drag their bedding outside the den, like housewives shaking blankets. Once when farsighted George and I were riding horseback in this pasture looking for cows, he spotted two baby foxes playing at a den entrance on the south side of this ridge. We told no one. We had neighbors who would even trespass on our land to shoot foxes or coyotes, as well as badgers.

Walking on the south side of the ridge later that day, I discover evidence of either a badger family castle or a lone badger with a liking for space. Several holes marked by piles of earth or gravel lie in a line a quarter mile long. With Frodo's help, I find bits of bloody bone, scraps of fur, blood, and matted grass nearby. I sit on a rock and contemplate the labor required to build such an incredible network. Perhaps the ridge is the ancestral stronghold of a badger family with older ties to this land than mine.

I add another phase to my dawn ritual. Before training the binoculars on the lake, I raise them to the hillside, trying to catch Badger returning from his night's hunt. I never have.

Not long after George died, I learned that badgers bury their dead. Like most bereaved, for a time I wished to be closer to George even if I had to die to do it. So I was intrigued to learn that badgers may wall up a dead mate inside an unused chamber. One naturalist once saw a sow badger emerge from a den uttering an eerie moan and begin digging in a nearby rabbit hole. Soon, a large boar arrived. The two touched noses, and the sow bobbed her head and made a whistling sound. The boar copied her. Both went into the den and emerged dragging a dead badger. Together, they maneuvered the corpse to the rabbit hole, stuffed it inside, and covered it with earth. When the female went back into her den, the male departed.

Other scientists have seen dead badgers pushed out of dens and covered with loads of bedding topped by earth and stones. One sow dug a ditch around her dead mate and his bed, throwing excavated dirt on top, tamping and smoothing. When she finished, the mound looked like a prehistoric round barrow grave.

Eavesdropping, I recently heard a woman tell another about a rancher who liked badgers and protected them on his ranch. After his death, his family found in his will specific instructions for the disposal of his body. They grumbled but carried out his wish: they cremated him and buried the ashes in a badger hole.

The phone is ringing when I finally limp up the front steps of Windbreak House. Every muscle aches from my fall into the badger hole. Yes, I reply to Mother, my doors and windows are locked. Yes, I checked the closets for burglars. We repeated similar lines every night since George's death.

If I don't answer Mother's sunset call, she stands at her back door shrieking until my father interrupts his chores and drives to my house. Using my hidden key, he comes inside and moves cautiously through the rooms, then reports to Mother that I am missing. All evening, they puzzle over the mystery, unable to imagine any reason I might go out at night. Mother putters in the kitchen, making the evening dishwashing last as long as possible so she can watch the entrance road through the window above the sink. If she sees my headlights approach, she runs into the driveway and waves until I stop and follow her inside. There I remind her that I stopped that morning to tell her about my appointment in town and left a note on their dining room table.

"She did not tell me," she says to my father, shifting stacks of old magazines and scratch paper from one side of the table to the other. "And I can't find any note. She's just trying to make me look forgetful."

"She shouldn't be out alone after dark anyway," my father says.

I've never settled in my mind whether "Early to bed, early to rise" is law or religion in my neighborhood. Females without male supervision are as rare as badgers and just as suspect. Stunned by widowhood, I am still relearning the habits of life alone, rediscovering my courage. My father gives orders I hardly notice, often doing what he suggests because it is simpler than thinking and I am numb with shock. Perhaps he feels responsible for me, and believes he has to tell me what to do because I have no other man to do it. Maybe his mind is already so impaired by strokes he thinks I am still a child.

Repeatedly, I remind my parents that most middle-aged women don't leave a daily itinerary with their parents. My father says, "Your mother worries about you," but I know my mother spends most evenings napping on the couch, secure in the knowledge that my father will fix anything that goes wrong.

After my parents' first phone call at dusk, I draw my shades to hide the house lights from anyone on the highway. Experience in traveling alone has taught me real danger might come by that route. Anyone who has car trouble in this valley would walk toward my lights. A man who learned I was alone might change from a supplicant to a danger. Inside the house, I am a mouse in a lighted cage. Hidden in darkness, anyone might watch me, might kick the glass out of a window and be upon me before I could escape.

After I draw the shades, I go outside again to walk my hillside. I've given up trying to explain to my parents how the prairie's darkness is safer than my house. Outside, the prairie's other citizens—coyotes, badgers, an occasional bobcat or mountain lion—are patrolling, doing their own sentry duty. I never fear the animals, who would slip silently around me, warned by their superior senses.

With the shades drawn, my house is invisible from a little distance. By curing my fear of the dark, I learned that after my eyes adjust I can see well by the light reflected into the grass by the stars or the moon. After a night walk I feel both serene and animated. Walking in darkness, even without George, I often think that without my parents' surveillance, I might live happily alone on this hilltop for the rest of my life.

Once or twice I have been startled by a shriek that cracks the darkness. Sounds common to daylight can be unsettling at night, but the din is neither coyotes nor owls, nor is it the mountain lion that travels the draw below my house. Maybe the big badger from the ridge was advertising his dominion.

Often, just as I drift off to sleep, I fantasize about skipping through the grass, warm winds blowing under a full moon. Perhaps the badger family is holding cotillions on the ridge above me, I think drowsily, picturing the old king badger at the entrance to his burrow, nodding his grizzled head. Sometimes as I lie listening to the night sounds on the pond—to frogs warbling, a killdeer calling questions—a duck squawks and splashes. By the time I raise my head, ducks are flapping into the sky as something large runs through the shallow water. I know that if I search in the morning, I'll find Badger's tracks amid broken turtle shells. Claw marks will reveal where he snatched a frog. Tumbled rocks and driftwood will show where he scratched for mice and moles. Splintered eggs. A few feathers. Just safeguarding his property, taking his compensation as the land's true lord.

I slide into sleep. At once the phone rings again. I lunge out of bed, stumbling through the dark house, to pick up the receiver, trembling.

"Just wanted to be sure you're in," my father says. "Sleep well, child."

Looking for Death:
The Deer Harvest

One sweaty June evening, hoping to find a cool breeze, Jerry and I
walked Frodo in a city park with a lake. As we followed the dog's slow
progress, I couldn't help talking about my father's erratic behavior, wish-
ing aloud that he were more like Jerry's grandfather, Rudolph.

The two men were nearly the same age and had similar family back-
grounds. Their grandfathers had emigrated from Sweden and Germany,
respectively, working awhile for relatives in Iowa to pay the debts of pas-
sage before homesteading near Hermosa, where the boys went to grade
school together. Rudolph later defied community and family tradition to
attend Black Hills State College in the northern Black Hills, instead of
staying with his brothers to work all their lives on the family farm. My
father also went to college, with help from his brothers and sisters,
because everyone believed that rheumatic fever had made him too weak
to do ranch work. He came back to the family ranch, eventually dividing
it with his brother Harold.

At twenty-one, Rudolph startled his family by marrying the college's
cook, a widow named Mary fourteen years his elder, and moving to her
small ranch in the northern Black Hills. Their daughter, Jerry's mother,
married in South Dakota but raised her children—Jerry and his brothers
and sister—in Oregon. Like most ranchers, both men hoped for a son or

grandson to take over the place. My parents tried and failed to have a child, hoping for a son.

When Rudolph's wife, Mary, died fifteen years ago, well-meaning acquaintances persuaded him to marry another widow. Her children and grandchildren filled his spare bedrooms with boyfriends, babies, dogs, and toys, and his outbuildings bulged with their cast-off belongings. Undistracted by the chaos, Rudolph set up a family corporation headed by his daughter, Jerry's mother. His second wife agreed to move back to her own house in town if Rudolph died first, taking the property she brought to the marriage and the appliances and furniture the couple bought together. Anything that originally belonged to Rudolph's first wife, along with the tools and farming equipment, was to be left on the ranch.

Jerry considered becoming a rancher when he lived with Rudolph for a couple of years after finishing high school. "All I learned," he says, shaking his head, "is that I didn't want to do that the rest of my life." He enrolled at Black Hills State during the one year I taught there. I met George that year, as well. Eventually, Jerry became an engineer and moved to Cheyenne. Still, his ties to his grandfather and to Rudolph's ranch are strong. We visited him together in the fall just before he died of cancer.

I admired Rudolph's good sense in weighing and deciding how his estate would be handled. I'd always assumed my father would make reasonable arrangements for his old age. Growing up, I compared my sensible father with his older brother, concluding Harold would be difficult and irascible in his old age. Instead, Harold worked out a plan to sell his ranch at a fixed price to the man who'd worked for him for years. My father wrapped himself in mindless rage.

Rudolph and John looked enough alike to be brothers. Both men stood tall and spare, their narrow faces and noble noses burned red by sun and wind. Both moved with amazing energy in their eighties.

Whenever I lost track of my dad on the ranch, I scanned the horizon for the bouncing pink of his faded red cap. Jerry says he could always find Rudolph the same way—his work cap is identical to my father's, faded to the same color. The first time I was inside Rudolph's barn, I could shut my eyes and find the tools and equipment he used most often—his one-legged milking stool, the can of bag balm for cows with sore teats— because my father kept the same things in the same places.

Following the elderly dog's dignified stroll, Jerry and I were both comfortable with long silences. We agreed that, despite our frustration in dealing with the two prickly old men, their teachings served us well. Both of us work hard at any task we tackle because we are products of the same stern upbringing. Finally, one of us mentioned the subject on both our minds, the last time we visited Rudolph's place together.

The biggest sin is sitting on your ass.

—FLORYNCE KENNEDY

Patience, shit.

—GEORGE WASHINGTON HAYDUKE,

in EDWARD ABBEY'S The Monkey Wrench Gang

Jerry comes out of the barn with a dead deer over his shoulder and drops it on the tailgate of Rudolph's pickup.

"Did you ever see anything like that? Why do you suppose he cut her legs off?" The old man gestures with his bloody knife at the doe's legs, hacked short above the knees. Normally, a hunter would slip a rope or the hook on an old singletree between the tendon and the leg bone, hanging the deer head down so the blood would drain, making skinning easy. This doe was hung by her neck from a rafter in the barn. Her purple tongue hangs out between bloody teeth.

Rudolph shakes his head, blue eyes snapping as he pushes the faded red cap back to scratch his head. When relatives of his second wife shot six deer on his farm last weekend and left them hanging in his barn, he called Jerry in Cheyenne and asked him to come up this weekend to butcher them. Temperatures stayed below freezing during the nights, and Rudolph shut the barn doors to keep dogs and coyotes out. During the day, the barn's dark interior kept the meat cool when temperatures outside hit forty degrees. Jerry is grumpy because he didn't get to hunt this year and is not anxious to cut up someone else's deer. But with this fall visit he's following a long tradition between him and his grandfather. Jerry has told me that once this job is done, Rudolph will probably work the conversation around to other chores he has saved to do with his grandson; it's his way of avoiding acknowledgment of his failing abilities.

Jerry drops his hatchet and knife sheath in the pickup bed and grabs a handful of hide on the deer's belly. Rudolph does the same, and they start skinning, as they've done together dozens of times.

Sitting on the side of the pickup box, I stretch as the sun warms my back and watch the two men work, noting that their resemblance is less in looks than in the smooth way they handle their knives in the exacting task of butchering. I set a pan and a bucket at my feet for the scraps and good meat they'll be tossing my way soon.

Beside the pickup, the old barn's siding glows in the afternoon sun, weathered silver-gray and streaked with gold pitch. Inside, singletrees scavenged from old wagons hang from rafters, swinging with the weight of does taken in the surrounding woods and fields. Rough, handmade milking stools lean against a stanchion. Old tools and cow medications crowd an orange-crate cupboard.

The old man's hands tremble and his knife blade wavers as he cuts hide away from the dark meat. At eighty-five, he is undergoing chemotherapy to treat cancer in his lungs, spine, and brain. He carves off a scrap of flesh pulverized by a bullet and throws it into the weeds south of the barn, shaking his head and muttering, "Cats'll eat good tonight."

A heavy gun booms nearby, once, twice. Rudolph glances toward a small field. "Sounds like somebody got one over by the road." Two more blasts follow, then another. "Maybe not." He grins, tossing away a bloody chunk of fat.

Jerry raises his head to listen as two more shots resound on the other side of the house. "Down at the bottom of the hill," he says. "Road hunting." He puts down his bowie knife and grabs the back of the deer hide with both hands. While Rudolph holds the sawed-off legs, Jerry peels the hide away, saying, "She's a little limp. Wish it had hung a few more days to dry out more—easier to cut."

"Getting too warm," Rudolph says, looking at the sky. "With the sun out, it might get up to fifty today."

"Besides, I'm here today," Jerry says. They grin at each other.

Jerry finishes stripping the hide off. With a hatchet, he chops off the deer's head and tosses it beside the barn. The doe's extended tongue is purple and covered with dust.

"I'll see how the females are doing," Rudolph murmurs, straightening slowly before he steps into the barn.

Jerry drops a couple of haunch roasts into the pan beside me. I start picking deer hair off them, but he shakes his head. "They'll have to wash them off anyway."

Just then a big blond woman in tight jeans and a bloody sweat-shirt emerges from the barn with a handful of meat strips. "Here's some jerky meat," she says, tossing it into the bucket. Jerry glances at it, shaking his head. "Easier to cut with the grain, and it dries better," he tells her.

"Can't we sell these hides someplace?" she asks. "Does anybody pay for them?" Jerry doesn't answer, and she turns back to the dark barn. Rudolph emerges with a handful of bloody meat. "Where does the jerky meat go?"

Jerry nods toward the bucket, but the old man sorts through the venison shreds in his hand, looking at the blood, straw, and hairs clinging to them. He glances into the barn, then tosses the mess into the weeds by the garage. Two magpies screech and fly up, startled away from their meal, then drop back to feed again.

Jerry cuts out the strips of meat along each side of the backbone, putting them gently in the pan. He glances up at me. "Hope we can get a few of those for breakfast steaks." He separates the ribs from the carcass and tosses them beside the barn next to the head. "No meat on a deer's ribs."

When the deer has been reduced to piles of crimson flesh, Rudolph drives the pickup to his "butchering shed," a storage building with a sturdy workbench at table height around two walls. The doors are open to dry the surfaces he scrubbed with disinfectant this morning. We crowd inside, and Rudolph drops onto a low bench in one corner. Jerry and I set the pans of meat on the counter and work side by side. Jerry cuts meat away from the shoulder and leg bones, putting them into another bucket with meat scraps to be boiled for stock. I pare gristle and sinew out of the dark flesh and mince it into one-inch chunks. Rudolph's wife will can the best meat for winter use, grinding and seasoning the rest for sausage or salami.

As the afternoon wanes, Rudolph sits telling tales of experiences with wildlife on this high point in the northern Black Hills. His voice warms the chilly shed, filling it with his vivid memories. As Jerry and I work, I am aware of being part of a timeless ritual, transforming this wild flesh into food that will nourish people in the long winter ahead.

"I told those Game, Fish and Parks boys a couple of years ago it was about time they had a doe season. There isn't anything running around up here but does and little spike bucks. All those hunters want these days is big trophies, so there isn't a decent buck left around. I think they're getting so inbred they aren't worth much. There isn't fifty pounds of meat on that doe," he says, pointing to the lean haunch Jerry is cutting.

Rudolph, who has lived on this hilltop for sixty years, points out that no doe season has been held in twenty or thirty. From his years of service on county weed, crop, and livestock committees, he knows too many deer damage forage and crowd other wildlife. Perhaps officials actually realized that he knew what he was talking about, or their own studies led to similar conclusions.

As Rudolph stares toward the sun, he says, "A couple of weeks ago, a fawn came out of the shelter belt over there, trotted through the yard gate and walked right up to the sliding glass doors. He looked in a minute, then browsed a little on the lawn before he went back to the trees. And another day I watched three does lay between the trees in the shelter belt for an hour." He pauses, plainly enjoying the sight again in his mind.

"A few days later some hunters came out, and I took them out to the end of that other shelter belt and told two of them to stand on the east side and told the third one to walk down the middle. In fifteen minutes, all three of them had does down not fifty feet from the barn." Smiling at the efficiency of this system, he seems no less pleased than when he spoke gently of the curious fawn and the resting does.

Rudolph picks up a bucket filled with meat and carries it to the house, shoulders stooping with the weight. When he returns, he drops two more haunches at Jerry's elbow.

"They said they're turning that whole deer into jerky," he reports, shaking his head. "Cutting every which way, across the grain, messing up nice pieces of meat."

"Shall we cut some steaks out of this back strap?" Jerry asks, holding up a thick rope of crimson venison. He has already wrapped some tiny steaks from another back strap for us, our mouths watering at the thought of breakfast venison.

"No, this one's just for sausage. It's Chuckie's deer," the old man says, naming one of his wife's grandsons.

Jerry drops his knife on the counter. "I'll cut meat for you, but Chuckie can cut up his own deer."

"Why don't you quit now?" Rudolph says smoothly, as if he hasn't heard. "We'll go shoot another one for steaks. I've got two more tags that haven't been filled. If those women are going to make jerky out of this, they can cut it up themselves."

Perhaps this is how he has remained serene as his second wife's family enveloped him. Lately, she has told everyone that the couple plans to move into a small house she owns in the nearby town. Jerry is worried that the old man will leave his farm and find himself completely confined, picked clean by bickering in-laws. But the talk has gone on for months, and Rudolph has not moved. Questioned about his intentions, he only smiles.

Rudolph takes another bucket of meat to the house, saying, "I'll get the rifle." I run ahead to open the door. In the kitchen, his wife is washing the canning jars and kettle. A daughter is banging drawers open and closed, piling jar lids on the counter. At the kitchen table, a heavyset granddaughter is chopping a slab of meat with a cleaver, grunting with each blow. Several children and dogs tumble through the living room.

Rudolph pours himself a cup of coffee and sits at the dining table. Calm in the middle of chaos, he gazes out the window toward his fields. His face looks gray. After a moment of rest, he's on the move again, heading outside with a smile. "We'll drive along the rim, then to the chokecherry patch and over by the spring. If there's any in there, we'll just wait until they come out, pick out a doe, and roll her over."

Jerry rolls his eyes at me and says quietly, "I don't suppose we'll even get out of the pickup. He's had a pretty long day."

West of the ranch buildings, the sun hovers just above Crow Peak, beginning its slide toward evening. Cool air swirls around us, sucked up from the canyon on the other side of the barn. "You drive, Jerry," Rudolph says, holding the rifle and gesturing me to the middle of the pickup seat. He slides in beside me. "This way I can shoot if we see one. Go down that trail past the barn and turn sharp left. Look down into that canyon by the barn. If they're in there, they'll come up on the rim right in front of us."

We drive past the barn, startling a half dozen magpies gobbling the meat scraps. Rudolph peers ahead, silhouetted against the late afternoon sun, an aging predator in a faded red wool cap, his arched nose like an eagle's beak. To my left, Jerry's face is bathed in gold light. He is smiling, perhaps recalling other evening drives with Rudolph.

"OK, now turn sharp right."

Truck tracks are plain in the tall grass and half-melted snow, and Jerry has followed this route often since he was a teenager, but Rudolph recites the directions anyway. He has covered this route with drivers who didn't have brains enough to follow a trail.

"Go on up to the top of this hill along the fence line now. You can go a little faster, because we won't see any here."

He points out a stack of round hay bales he says weigh nine hundred pounds apiece, then gestures toward the next field, where shoots four inches high are so uniformly green they look like the fake grass on a miniature golf course. "That winter wheat is looking pretty good. If we get a little moisture in the spring, it'll really pop because it's got a good start. I got fifty bushels off there last year."

He falls silent, perhaps thinking how some neighbors criticized him for pouring labor and money into terraces on his dry upland place. But the contours catch and hold every drop of moisture that falls here. His crops are better, and the grass is deep enough to hide a standing deer.

"Now drive along the lower side of this terrace. Sometimes they lay up on the topside, so they can see down toward the road and the shelter belt. If they're up there, they'll stand up and we can pop one."

Jerry follows tire tracks in the snow along the terrace, but it is soon apparent that no deer will stand. We scan a shelter belt on the west side of the wheat field, too far for a successful shot. On the other side of it, a pickup moves slowly, road hunters making a last sweep before sunset. Across the road stand three new houses and a fourth half finished, its huge panes of glass reflecting sunset. Some of Rudolph's neighbors are selling land for housing developments.

"OK," says Rudolph, "now cross right there where the tracks are and go up that hill right into the corner of the fence and then turn sharp left and put her in super low and drive real slow toward the chokecherry patch."

On the road, the other pickup's lights move parallel with ours. Crow Peak looms black and jagged in the southwest, casting a deep shadow as the sun moves lower.

"Now you just put her in super low," Rudolph says, "and just creep as slow as you can over this hill. If they're in there, they'll come out above the bushes and look back at us for a minute. With that hill behind them, I don't have to worry about where the bullets are going if I miss."

Barely moving, the pickup grumbles over the hill, and we stare down into a patch of chokecherry bushes. At first, the hill looks serene: golden brown bushes blend with gray patches of limestone, little drifts of snow, matted tawny grass. Then my eyes focus on two deer heads, great creamy ears turned toward the pickup.

As my mouth forms the word, "Deer," my brain protests: If he shoots, we'll have to skin another one tonight. The two does leap out of the bushes and pause broadside, perfect targets, staring.

Rudolph stands beside the pickup, sighting across the open passenger door. "Does," he says and his .308 makes a small, flat, report. Hearing it, I don't believe a bullet that sounds so quiet can possibly kill the big animals. One deer leaps and falls, then staggers to her feet and stumbles over the hill. The other simply turns and vanishes. Rudolph is back inside the truck, holding the door. Jerry swings the steering wheel hard left and accelerates, muttering, "This isn't hunting. It's harvest."

Rudolph yells, "Stop!" As the truck halts, he is already sighting on a deer emerging from a low gully on the next slope. She stops, looking back.

Jerry says quietly, "Wait!" At the same time I say, "That's not the same deer." The rifle snaps again. The deer whirls, beginning a leap that ends in a flat fall. I blink and the white belly fur becomes only another patch of snow on the hillside, invisible. Rudolph glances at us, smiling.

"That's not the same deer," I say again. Jerry turns off the ignition and gets out of the truck. "You drive, help him. I'll go after the wounded one." He reaches for the rifle.

"What?" Rudolph says, getting obediently into the passenger seat.

"You shot two deer, Deadeye." I start the pickup and shift into low. "The second time you shot, it was the other deer. You dropped that one clean. Jerry's going after the first one."

"Oh," says Rudolph. Several emotions flow over his face. He directs me down the hill and around the end of a snow-packed gully where the deer lies. I stare at the animal, watching for any movement. Without looking at her, Rudolph says, "It's gone. Get up where Jerry is."

"Aren't we supposed to cut its throat to be sure?" I ask.

He glances toward the deer. "It's dead," he says again and motions toward the hilltop. As we head toward Jerry, we see that he is studying the ground. He takes one step and begins to raise the rifle, then steps forward again. The doe materializes on the hillside right in front of him and makes a scrambling run, ducking under a fence. Jerry fires as the pickup hits a bump. When I look again, the doe has crossed a little hill and disappeared. The light is fading fast as the sun's upper edge finally slips behind Crow Peak. Jerry reaches the fence, puts the rifle down to climb over, then picks up the rifle and follows the deer out of sight over the hill.

"Let's go back and get that other one loaded before it gets any darker," Rudolph directs, frowning. "Then we can help him look."

A neat red hole just behind the deer's shoulder shows that Rudolph's shot was perfect, "in the lights," he says. A tiny blood pond lies by her nose. Her eyes are open. Surreptitiously, I feel her throat for a pulse, then remember the abrupt, loose-jointed fall. Jerry told me once, "The eyes of every dead deer I've seen have been open and its head flat on the ground. When I've walked up on one that was alive, its eyes were shut and sometimes its head up."

With both of us lifting, the deer seems light as she swings up over the tailgate, but the body fills the pickup bed. As her head flops, blood splashes up, a gobbet striking my lips. I try to wipe it away with a bloody mitten, but the rich, salty taste fills my tongue. I'm surprised when my mouth waters.

When we get back in the pickup, Rudolph slides behind the wheel. "I know where the gate is," he explains, switching on the headlights. Jerry is out of sight. Rudolph leans forward, his wrinkled face thin and set under his faded red hat, peering into the shadows. The headlights make the surrounding land darken and gather around us. He peers into the shadows.

We leave the gate open and drive to the top of a hill Jerry crossed following the doe. The slope is snowy, but ahead of us are low, regular tan heaps that look unnatural. "Sawdust," Rudolph explains. "The sawmill needs someplace to dump it, so this neighbor leased them this piece. They say eventually it breaks down."

The mounds are several feet thick in spots, wet with melted snow, like a moonscape. "But it will kill the grass," I say.

Rudolph grins at me like a teacher proud of a pupil. "He's old, can't run cattle anymore. No one to leave the place to but a nephew who's talking about selling out for development."

On the far side of the field with its strange crop, I spot Jerry walking steadily toward a belt of trees and gesture to be sure Rudolph sees him. "Do you suppose the doe lay down in those trees?"

Rudolph shakes his head. "I'll bet that doe went straight through those trees and into Beets Canyon. Unless she collapsed pretty close there, he'll never find her now, getting dark."

He honks to summon Jerry, who is looking doubtfully at the tangled brush and trees ahead of him. "You know, that canyon's always just full of hunters. Deer come running out of it in all directions during deer season."

I glance over my shoulder. Crow Peak is black, outlined in gold as the sun sinks.

"Just walk up to where that lone pine stands on the edge of the canyon, Jerry," Rudolph yells out the window. "If she got further than that, you won't find her anyway."

The pickup idles, moving slowly along the edge of the canyon. I stare hard, hoping to see the deer.

"I had a guy come hunting out here once, asked me where to get a deer," Rudolph says. "I told him to go sit under that lone pine and just wait, somebody hunting down in the canyon would chase one past him. About a half hour he was back, said somebody was shooting at him. Shot a branch over his head and it dropped down, and he thought he was shot. He was shaking."

He glances at me. "Some of those fellows don't pay any attention to where they're shooting. I told him to go back out in the corner of this field, stay in his truck, and a deer would come along there. They go every direction out of that canyon trying to get away. About another half hour he was back with a deer in the back of his outfit." He waves at Jerry, who turns back at the pine and begins walking toward us. "Look at that view."

I say, "You've had the best view in the Hills," before realizing I'm using the past tense. He may not know I've been told about his cancer. Trying to cover the error, I blurt, "You've had a pretty good day. Got three deer, a youngster to help you skin 'em, and a bunch of women to can them and cook them up for you."

In my mind an ancient story has been unfolding behind the modern one: The aged king has killed with one shot, confirming his eyesight and abilities as a warrior, proving one more time his right to reign over his empire. He's watched his young disciple and found his skills satisfactory as he tracked the wounded deer. Rudolph's triumph is not diminished because Jerry hasn't found the game. All day I've felt as if we were all three performing a stately ceremony in these familiar autumn jobs. My bloody lips remind me of how our ancestors celebrated a successful harvest of provisions for winter, restoring their strength by drinking warm blood and eating raw liver.

The old man is looking at me and speaking, so I wonder what I've missed. "I wish I'd had the guts to buy more land around here, keep people from building all those houses. But I'd have had to borrow money for that. I couldn't do it."

The ranch has not always provided Rudolph and his families with enough to sustain them, so he often took other jobs. With his first wife, he ran a boarding house in town, then worked on bridge construction, as a carpenter, and at a gas station. But he did more than survive. He plowed labor and income back into the land, planning for its future, not necessarily his own. In recent years, strength waning, he's been unable to repair his sheds and corrals as well as he once did, but his granary is tight, his tools neatly arranged. He's encouraged his neighbors to resist the easy riches of selling out to developers, to keep the area rural.

Jerry has reached the pickup. "We might as well forget it," Rudolph says. "It's too dark to see anything. Maybe those road hunters picked her up."

"I followed a blood trail for a while after she jumped the fence, but I didn't see any as I crossed the field," Jerry says, reluctant to leave. As Rudolph drives back across the pasture, they agree that hunting in the dark is useless and that the deer is probably dead.

"Can't we come back in the morning?" I ask. "It'll be cold tonight, and we'll probably see her right away when we can follow tracks in daylight."

Rudolph shakes his head. "Meat'll be spoiled. Hot, all that running, blood left in it all night."

Jerry nods, getting out to shut the gate. I follow him, feeling an urgency I can't explain but reluctant to argue with their experience. Surely the deer is dead, but I don't believe she went as far as the canyon. I'm drawn toward the sawdust mounds. As my eyes adjust to dusk's light, I'm able to see more detail than I could behind the pickup's headlights.

"What if she turned south right after she crossed the fence?" I ask Jerry. "I have a strong feeling she's closer to the fence than we were looking. She was hurt bad."

"I didn't go far that way," Jerry admits. "I thought she'd run right for the canyon."

I shake my head. "I don't think she had the strength. There's enough light to look a little more. If we both walked south, we might see her."

"Too dark," Rudolph mutters. "Can't see a thing."

"Let me just look in the sawdust," I say, walking quickly away from the pickup, hoping Rudolph won't drive off. "Just a few minutes."

Jerry drops the gate, snatches the rifle, and follows. Rudolph turns the pickup toward us. I dodge around the end of one mound of sawdust, trying to escape the lights' glare, and Rudolph stops. "Don't want to drive into a big pile of that stuff. Probably get stuck," I hear him say.

Jerry and I walk fast, turning our heads from side to side, scanning low spots, now pooled in shadow. We examine each patch of snow for drops of blood. In a few minutes, I am walking rapidly without having to look at my feet, just as if I knew this ground. I don't stumble. I feel as if I could walk all night without touching the ground. The afterglow on Crow Peak dims.

The pickup's headlights flash as Rudolph swings one way, then the other. Jerry has moved ahead, walking the edge of a low ravine, but he is just a man-shaped silhouette, turning toward me now, giving up. We've done our best. Suddenly I understand why even careful hunters are sometimes guilty of the unthinkable: leaving a wounded animal.

Ahead, across a narrow fold in the hill, I see a gray mound, probably a bush. I decide to be sure before I quit and plod back to the pickup. Three steps down the slope, I realize the snowdrift I am about to step on is white belly fur: the doe lies at my feet. I lay my hand on her neck, not to feel for a pulse. Her eyes are open, snow scuffed between her legs, as if she was trying to run as she fell.

I try to call, but no sound comes out. Deep breath. Try again. "Here she is!"

Jerry's footsteps stop. "You found her?" he says, closer than I thought. "Dead?"

"Yes. Right after she crossed the fence."

He hands me the rifle, draws his knife, and slits the belly open. Reaching inside to pull the entrails out, he grimaces. "Grass all over in here. That bullet must have torn everything up. Whew." A strong smell, like rotting grass, rises with steam from the doe's belly.

I can't see the rifle in my hands as I walk toward the skyline, finding the pickup by its silhouette. Rudolph is sitting in the dark cab, a cigarette glowing. He flinches when I get in.

"Found her, back that way."

He nods. "Dead?" But he knows the answer.

"Yes, probably right away."

"Get in and show me," he says, jaw line relaxing. Looking out at the dark through the pickup windshield, I am suddenly lost, the harsh light across the sawdust and grass utterly unlike the soft shadowy world where I found the deer. The ground slopes before us, and the headlights hit Jerry, bloody to the elbows, emptying the deer's belly.

Rudolph aims the lights toward the work, and I drag the first deer out of the pickup box and over beside the second. Jerry moves over to begin gutting her.

The old man leans on the pickup breathing harshly, but his voice is controlled. "Did you get the hearts? I love baked heart."

I hesitate an instant, then pull my knife and reach into the organs Jerry has piled between the carcasses. I cut both hearts loose and carry them steaming in a chill wind to Rudolph. He pulls a plastic bag from a coat pocket, shakes it briefly, and flips the meat into it.

"How about the livers?" he says. I can barely see his grin as I plunge my hands back into the hot innards. "Do you know deer don't have a gall?" he says.

I forgot puncturing a beef gall could ruin the liver. Perhaps this is Rudolph's gentle way of reminding me. "No," I say, turning toward him, "I didn't know that." My shirt and arms are covered with blood. I drop one liver in his bag, adding, "The other one's all torn up." He nods.

The smell of blood is nearly overpowering, but we smile as we get back in the truck. On the slow drive home, all three of us admire the deer's guile in turning so swiftly, getting down into a low spot so she couldn't be seen.

Rudolph finds the gate and starts to open his door, then slumps as Jerry gets out to shut it. At the barn, we drag both deer inside, rig singletrees and pulleys. I pull on a rope while the men lift, until the does are hanging off the floor.

"Oh, yeah," says Rudolph. "I guess I better do this." He draws two yellow tags out of his pocket and fastens one to a leg of each doe.

"I forgot you had tags," I say.

"I wouldn't say I've always had tags," he says, grinning, "but I do this time." We all stand a moment, breathing hard.

In a moment, Rudolph will turn off the lights and lead us toward the house in icy darkness. He says, "That's the last deer that will be hanging in this barn."

When the silence has lasted an instant too long, Jerry glances at his grandfather.

"Until next year," Rudolph adds.

But that's not what he means.

The Young Cow:
Going Back
to Grass

Not long after we helped Rudolph butcher the deer, he was admitted to the hospital. I went with Jerry to visit him, restlessly pacing the halls until most of the relatives and friends left. When I looked into the room, Jerry was sitting beside the bed. Rudolph glanced at me, nodded, and went on talking quietly. He reminded Jerry of the trust he had arranged so that his daughters—Jerry's mother and her half-sister—will own the land during their lifetimes. Then Rudolph described, precisely and in detail, how his farm might be run to the land's best advantage for the next twenty years. He itemized the repairs needed and suggested crops to plant, outlined choices the family might make if the neighborhood continues to exchange farms for housing tracts. He repeated his hope that the farm wouldn't be sold for development or turned into another hobby farm, but acknowledged that the decision would belong to his daughters and their descendants.

After Rudolph's funeral, I helped Jerry clean out the farmhouse and buildings for renters. Resting, he sat in the chair at the kitchen table where the old man sat the day we shot the deer. I remembered Rudolph's smile as he looked outside. Jerry's face was hard, his face blank.

That day, the kitchen table and chair were the only furnishings left in the house. Stove, refrigerator, beds, linens, pictures—everything had vanished. His grandmother's silverware was gone, along with antique canning jars. No toilet paper, no soap or towels. Even the ancient, half empty bottle of bourbon Rudolph kept in a tiny cupboard in the bathroom for hot toddies when he felt a cold coming on was gone.

Outside, the yard was a mess, and buildings bulged with trash. The day we'd butchered the deer, Rudolph had offered Jerry his collection of antique wooden tools, his bamboo fishing poles. Jerry refused to take Rudolph's cherished things while the old man was alive. Now he was angry, believing they were gone with everything else, until I admitted hiding them under a hay bale in the barn.

Rudolph moved to this farm when he was twenty-one years old, and found several pairs of ox shoes, remnants of the Cheyenne-to-Deadwood trail, as he worked the fields. He nailed them to the barn, where they weathered for sixty years. Gone.

Jerry sat at the table, drinking coffee from a thermos, looking out the window at his grandfather's land. I leaned against the wall behind him. Will my father sell the ranch as he threatens, empty our house and our lives of the past?

Outside the window, the shelter belt looked the same as it did the day Rudolph told us about the fawn walking up to the glass doors. Somewhere among the trees, deer grazed. The pale green fields rolled away to the blue-black base of Crow Peak, immobile and serene.

As for man

his days are as grass:

as a flower in the field,

as he flourisheth.

For the wind passeth over it

and is gone;

and the place thereof

shall know it no more.

—PSALM 103:15–16, copied into

John Hasselstrom's 1985 journal

I bequeath myself to the dirt to grow from the grass I love,

If you want me again look for me under your boot-soles.

—WALT WHITMAN

"Song of Myself"

One hot day in early July, I make my weekly drive north, from Cheyenne to the ranch. When I get to my hilltop house, I realize I've broken my routine by failing to stop at my parents' house. Instead of going back, I climb the railroad-tie fence George built on top of the hill, settling on the top rail. Looking at my windbreak trees with the sun behind me, I relax against the warmth as if I were sitting on George's lap.

Is my father, as he ages, simply becoming more traditional, sliding back into the habits he learned as a child? His father moved onto these grasslands, a region completely alien to his Swedish homeland, almost a hundred years ago. He had been a cobbler, but he taught himself how to ranch in a way that sustained the native grasses and wildlife as well as his cattle. Somehow, when ranchers all around him were taking the advice of agricultural experts, borrowing money to buy machinery to plow every acre they owned, he resisted the pressure. He must have been a careful student of the land and his cattle, noticing how native species of grass thrived in aridity and tough conditions. Only in the rich bottoms did he plow for alfalfa and other non-native plants. He irrigated only when the creek flooded, used gently contoured ditches to spread water slowly.

Following that cobbler's teachings, my father has stubbornly managed to sustain this ranch, while sharing the land with the antelope and coyotes and grouse, with buffaloberry and plum. All over the nation, experts and environmentalists, economists and ecologists acknowledge that the Great Plains is about to suffer a physical and financial disaster worse than the drought of the Dirty Thirties. Plowing the thin dry soil has created dust storms and areas barren of growth. Environmentalists deplore the loss of virgin prairie and the species that have dwelled there. Our ranch is an exception.

A saying among ranchers is that the only way to afford a ranch these days is to inherit, or marry it. Many ranchers, facing taxes at a higher rate than the land can possibly produce, sell out. If I were part owner of the ranch, I might manage to deflect enough of the inheritance taxes to keep it. Development is moving down from the mountains, causing land valuations and taxes to rise. If my father sells our ranch, as he threatens, the new owner will have to borrow money to buy and may never recoup his investment. If he wants to run cattle or buffalo on the land, he may overstock, trying to raise and sell enough cattle to reduce his debt quickly. Overgrazing would, in turn, degrade the land, make it worth less in the real-world terms of what it will sustain, even while the price to purchase it, and the taxes, go up.

My father says the ranch has given him a good living, but my parents have scrimped all their lives. A few years back, they admitted having used a savings account left me by an aunt to pay off purchase of some hay land. Perhaps my father's mind is affected not only by the natural deterioration of age and damage from strokes, but by something more.

He has always been "tight as the bark on a tree," a habit he must have learned from his father, along with his practice of keeping a journal. Karl Hasselstrom—who Americanized his name to Charles and forbade his children to learn Swedish—devoted two pages in his journal to each month's income and expenses. On the left page, he noted every penny made, so I know he sold potatoes for fifty cents on April 20, 1904. On the opposite page, he recorded expenses such as ten cents for stove polish on April 23 of the same year.

A generation later, my father keeps the same kind of records. He has always argued with my mother and me over everything we wanted or bought. He knows our costs, even for necessities, have risen more quickly than our income from cattle sales. He knows the life he has left is shorter than the time he has spent. Every day he grows shorter tempered, confused by the details of modern living— automatic cash machines, recorded voices when he calls the bank. Surely he fears losing control where he has always ruled, here on the ranch. He is failing even to care for his cattle and must realize he can't blame me or modern technology.

Why didn't he plan, as Rudolph did, for the decline that he has always known might come in old age? Is there another cause for his rage? He has never discussed money with me, but he may know that pinching pennies will no longer be enough to pay the expenses of this ranch, or any other. Is he angry because he is afraid he will lose it no matter what he does?

On each return to the ranch, I talk to my mother and other relatives about the stranger my father has become, asking their help. Some shrug and say, "He's just like he always was, except a little meaner." Occasionally, someone nods sagely and says, "You have to make the decision." What decision? I've thought of a dozen possibilities, even talked to my lawyer, and I have no power other than persuasion. When I try to talk reason to my mother, she tells everyone I am "just exaggerating again." George taught me bad habits, she says, like disobeying my parents. My father tells Harold that writing has muddled my brain. I'm off gadding about when Mother needs me. Good thing, he adds, that George died before he ruined me for life.

I shift my thigh away from a nail, recalling how George and I came to build this fence. He'd noticed how many crooked or broken ties railroad workers discarded along the railroad tracks to the east. They were a hazard to the horses when we rode in the right of way, and if they caught fire, they burned for days. So he started loading a few on the pickup each time we crossed the tracks, stacking them on the hillside. The completed fence, more than ornamental, caught snow that would otherwise blow into our driveway, allowing it to melt slowly and provide moisture for the windbreak. When I teased George that he'd built a fort, he nodded. "We'd have a good field of fire from here. Hard to sneak up on." Scratching his beard, he added, "If we strung concertina wire, would that keep your folks from hiking up here every day?"

Still reluctant to go down to my parents' house, I walk among the trees, wishing George could see how much they've grown. I feel as if my parents' lives are deteriorating while I watch from behind a thick glass window. I begin and end each day trying to decide what to do. Right now, I itch to get my fencing tools and start tightening loose strands of wire in the driveway fence, but I know the impulse is only a desire to busy myself with physical work so I can't think. So far I refuse to admit I can do nothing to help my father. I keep driving back and forth between Cheyenne and the ranch, hoping I will be here for the final crisis, whenever and whatever it is.

I stomp a few times beside a tree and kick the trunk to alert any dozing rattlesnakes. Then I push the long grass aside and lift a slab of old carpet I used as mulch, following Margaret's recommendations, and prod the soil with a finger. Damp enough so I won't have to water until my next visit.

A bobbing pink speck in the tan prairie catches my eye: my father, in his faded cap, walking up the hill. I turn my back, dreading a quarrel.

A few days after George died, I was working in the windbreak, when I noticed my father approaching. I kept stacking magazines around the trees, weighing them down with rocks. Besides eliminating clutter inside the house, I was killing weeds before they sprouted. When my father got close, I stretched and faced him.

"You've made quite a start on a windbreak here," he said. Tipping his head back to look up, he added, "I didn't realize these trees are as tall as I am."

I nodded. "Our work is starting to pay off. This irrigation hose George laid helped a lot. Look at the buffaloberries and plums— first year they've borne fruit."

Showing him how the magazines, held in place by rocks and scraps of carpet, smothered weeds and funneled water to each tree, I led him away from a particular row so he wouldn't notice his old coats. For years Mother had refused to wash his work clothes if they had blood or manure on them, so he kept a couple of ragged coats and coveralls in the barn to wear during calving season. I had gotten him a new winter coat and coveralls at Christmas that year, washing them myself when they needed it. If he'd known I was using the old coats as mulch, he'd have yanked them out from under my trees and hung them back in the barn.

My father studied the snaky black lines of drip hoses as we waded through waist-deep grass to the hill's west side, where the bushes were big enough to catch snow in the winter, irrigating their own roots. I watered the surrounding grass enough to keep it green and slow down a prairie fire. And with the windbreak coming along, I hoped that its trees would muffle motor noise from the highway, where traffic increases every year.

"You've made quite a home place out of this bare hillside," he said, smiling. His lips puckered as he bit into an orange plum. "I believe this is the first fruit ever raised on this place." I watched his face to see if he was kidding. We'd always picked plums and apples in the front yard. "Didn't we used to drive the cattle out of this hole in snow storms?"

I waved at a cluster of junipers nearer the house. "Those trees are twice as tall as the others because they're planted in the manure the cows left when they waited out those blizzards." We stood together for a moment, knee deep in grass, looking down over the home place.

"You know," I said, "when we had this surveyed, we found out none of these trees are on the five acres you deeded to me. In fact, the house isn't completely on that acreage. And you know the county considers anything under forty acres nonagricultural land, so my taxes doubled this year. Could I buy another thirty-five acres from you?"

Abruptly, his manner changed. "You're already making more money out of this ranch than I am." His mouth was tight, as if he hadn't finished the plum. "And don't think I didn't notice how you had the sale ring write a separate check to you when we sold the calves. Behind my back."

"They should have been writing separate checks ever since my brand was registered and I started selling cows. My accountant says otherwise that money appears to be wages."

He looked down at me, eyes chilly blue. "I don't need an accountant to know you did it so you wouldn't have to pay for all the work and feed I put into your cattle."

I inhaled slowly, feeling my face redden but determined to keep the fury out of my voice. "Last time we talked about this, you said my cattle and the money they bring are my pay for being here in the winter. Without the cows, I wouldn't have income to offset my expenses here."

He started walking away. "You better keep your cows. You could starve to death on what you make writing."

Hurrying like a child to catch up with him, I said, "I don't have George's income now. I have to make more money just to pay the taxes."

"I'll write you a check right now." He stopped and cocked his head to look at my house, his thumbs in his back pockets. "Ten thousand bucks. Good price for a house."

"You can't buy my house!" Deep breath. "Anyway, it's assessed at sixty-five. But that's not the point." I gritted my teeth and spoke calmly. "If you sell me another thirty-five acres, my place will be classed as ag land and the taxes will be low enough so I can make enough money writing and teaching to pay them and still eat."

"You just want my place." With his back to the sun, he eyed the house. "Tell you what. Since you want money, I'll give you fifty thousand dollars right now. You sign away any claim to the ranch. Then you leave and never come back." The sun shone so bright on his back I couldn't see his expression, just his black silhouette.

I took another deep breath. "I'm not talking about leaving. I'm trying to explain my financial situation to you, so we can work out a compromise," I said slowly. "I've already spent half my life here. I plan to be here the rest of it."

"You're trying to steal my ranch." He stepped away from me.

"How could your own daughter steal your ranch?" In spite of my resolution to stay calm, my voice rose. "Who else would you leave it to?"

"I can do whatever I want with it. Fifty thousand." He slapped his back pocket. "I've got my checkbook right here. Take it and get out or shut up and do what I tell you. Quit wasting time writing that drivel and maybe we can get some work done around here." He started walking across the hilltop.

"I'll work with you," I said, "but I want to be a partner, not a hired hand." I stumbled, trying not to collide with him as he stopped abruptly. "And I'm not likely to quit writing now."

"If you don't want the ranch," he said, "I might as well sell it." He took several long strides through the grass.

"I want the ranch," I yelped. "This is my home."

His red cap bounced as he marched down the hill, dust puffing under his worn work shoes. I sat down on the railroad-tie fence to watch him. Sunset cast my shadow across his path. He sauntered over it and disappeared behind the corral fence. He was so thin he looked fragile, but his straight back looked as it had for the past forty years. Like the badger, he always left with deceptive speed. After he vanished, I sat awhile on the fence with my eyes shut, trying to remember the clasp of George's arms around me. The same night, Harold called to say, "Your dad tells me you're selling your house and you want him to sell the ranch."

This time my father is walking up the hill to ask if I'll drive him over east. When he went to that pasture this morning, he found a cow unable to get up, and he wants to look at her again. I immediately check to be sure that George's .357 is tucked beside my .45 pistol under the seat of my Bronco, and talk my father into riding with me. He consents, but he won't let me turn on the air conditioning. Heat wavers on the hood. He doesn't speak for several miles, restlessly turning his pockets inside out until he finds a tiny bottle.

"Got these when your mother and I went to the Mayo clinic," he says, holding the bottle up so I can read the label: nitroglycerin. "After that time—was that last month?—when my stomach was bothering me and you put me in the hospital." He grins at me as he used to when we shared a joke.

"I don't really need them, but I've been wondering how they taste." He puts one under his tongue while I read the label and tell him they are only for emergencies. Almost immediately, he grimaces and rolls down the window to spit it out. "Tastes terrible," he says. "Why would they give me junk like that?"

I'm driving down the long slope toward the spring in the summer pasture when he speaks again. "I didn't want to say it in front of your mother, but you picked a good time to be here. Don't like to handle a gun when I'm alone, you know, but I hated to think of her suffering in this heat." He lifts his cap and scratches his head. "Dammit, I forgot to bring my .22."

The young Hereford cow lies with her legs tucked under her on a grassy bench. Her head is up, ears pricked. She faces us as I park ten feet away. Surrender shines in her eyes, clear as when I saw it in the eyes of the first animal I killed, the sick steer thirty-five years ago. For a year after I dragged it to the bone yard, I looked away each time I passed his carcass. This cow can decompose where she lies. The scavengers already know where to find her. A pink balloon under her tail bulges into rolls of shredded flesh and digested grass. Coyotes' tracks mark a pool of blood around her back legs. A four-month-old calf lies with his head against her flank.

"A good young cow," Father says, looking away. "I thought she was just resting until I got over on this side of her. Ugh."

The calf stands and stretches, then kneels in blood beside the cow's belly and wraps his tongue around a nipple sticking up from her swollen udder.

"Makes me sick to see that," Father says. "Do you suppose we could get her home? Maybe a vet could sew her up and we could keep her alive until she raised the calf. Sell her in the fall."

"Coyotes have eaten part of her stomach. See where the grass slopped out?" I unzip the .357 case and open it on my lap. The barrel shines blue against the sheepskin lining, smudged by one big thumbprint. I haven't used the pistol since George cleaned it. I thank him one more time for teaching me—physically and mentally—how to handle this weapon. I learned how to shoot when I got my .22 rifle. George taught me how to kill if I had to.

Father rubs his chin. "How could we load her? Maybe bring the tractor over here to lift her into the pickup."

"She'd lay here another four or five hours in this heat. Her guts are already rotting. Bound to be infection." I flip the chamber open: six heavy shells.

Father leans forward. "George's pistol? Ugly thing, isn't it?" Frowning, he picks up the leather strap full of squat bullets. "Jesus. They're monsters."

"Hollow points. FBI told George these are just for killing." I put the case down on the seat.

He extends his hand. "How do you load it? Does it kick much?"

"Like a mule," I say, casually switching hands on the pistol to keep it away from him. "It's loaded—all six chambers." I slip two more bullets into the back pocket of my jeans and hold the pistol left-handed, barrel pointing up, as I open the door.

"Isn't that kinda dangerous?" he says, leaning back against the door.

"I carry it for protection. I don't want to hear a click on an empty chamber if I have to shoot somebody."

Father fumbles with the seat belt latch as I slide out and ease toward the cow. "Maybe we better go back to the house so I can get my rifle. I'm used to that," he says. "Let me try a few shots at that cottonwood tree first."

The cow lifts her head and widens her nostrils but relaxes as she inhales my familiar scent. The calf turns to look at me, his tongue dripping milk, hanging out between his teeth. When I wave, he trots twenty feet away. A swarm of flies buzzes up from the cow's open wound.

I take three more steps and extend the pistol so the barrel rests against a white curl in the center of the cow's forehead. She leans forward to sniff and lick my boot.

"Sorry, lady," I murmur. "Go back to grass." Wrist relaxed, I pull the trigger. Her head drops to her curled foreleg. The blackened hole is the size of my thumb.

From the corner of my eye, I see Father's head jerk up. "Christ!" He yanks the seat belt loose and swings the door open.

Leaning forward, I place the pistol barrel at the corner of the cow's eye and fire again. The sound is flat. She doesn't move.

"My God," says my father close behind me. I step away from the cow to eject the smoking shells and reload. He nudges her nose with the toe of his shoe. When I look up, he has backed away to lean against the pickup door, his face rigid as a cedar post.

"Right here OK for her?" I ask.

His jaw twitches. "What?" He glances at the pistol. "Oh, this is a good place for her. She's above high water. The coyotes can come back and finish the job."

He gets behind the wheel, so I slide in the passenger door, putting the pistol on the seat between us. He stares at it until I zip the case shut, then grinds the ignition as he starts the car. "Can you come back over with me in the morning?" he asks as he shifts, and I nod. "We'll bring your horse in the trailer and haul the calf home. I've got a cow in the corral with enough milk to feed six calves his size. I've been tying her up anyway, because I have another orphan in the shed. She's getting pretty agreeable about it."

He doesn't speak again until we start down the last long hill before reaching the ranch. A long sweep of grass stretches to the ranch buildings, tips of the blades gold in the sun.

"Remember that book by Faulkner you read in school—is it *The Mansion*? Anyway, Mink Snopes gets out of prison after forty years. He lies down on the ground. He can feel it drawing him down, and he wants to go." The Bronco idles to a stop as he looks off across the prairie. "Down into the grass."

Looking for the Light: The Elk in the Aspen

The night before my forty-ninth birthday, I dreamed of opening a shallow, clean box filled with bones. I recognized the bones as those from George's arms and legs. In the dream I wept, lifting the skeletons of his big hands, rubbing my fingertips over the coarse texture. He always apologized for his rough skin, but his touch was gentle. As I placed each bone on a wool blanket, my rational mind reminded me that the skeleton inside George's coffin would not be so immaculate as the bones in my hands. Even cattle carcasses scoured by plains weather and picked by vultures and coyotes retain bits of rotten flesh and ragged sinew. The sweet bone-gathering fantasy ended.

But at once I was flying through the air wearing sturdy straps around my chest, waist, legs, and ankles. For a moment I forgot my fear of heights and admired a carnival from above, secure and unafraid. The pressure of the straps increased until I struggled to breathe. I soared higher, sweeping through a great crescent.

Rrrrrip! A Velcro fastening parted. I looked down. A strap around one ankle trailed loose. More straps ruptured as I dangled, watching: first my ankles were free, then my legs. The straps around my chest held me so tightly I wheezed.

I knew at the end of my next arc, gravity would snatch me clear, spin me out beyond the stars. Free of the ranch, I thought, free of my father, but flying out of control into darkness.

Human beings meet for a moment in the reaches of time and space, trailing sparks like comet's hair—but we belong to ourselves. We are all required at last to accept full responsibility for our own events and conditions, and only so long as we evade it, crying after some other arrangement, are we fragmented, lost, unquiet, unloved.

—Advice to a Young Wife from an Old Mistress

When I wake from the dream, it's nearly dawn. I smell coffee, so I know Jerry is already downstairs. I got back from the ranch late last night because saving the orphan calf turned into an ordeal that took all day. My dirty clothes are still in my suitcase, but Jerry and I are leaving for Jackson Hole in an hour. I'm teaching two writing workshops to earn a little money while he spends the days fishing. I empty the suitcase into the hamper and then haul it to the closet. As I sort out the clothes I'll need, I wonder if my father remembers the orphans, and what will happen at the ranch while I'm gone.

Jackson Hole has lured tourists since the first human, probably wearing greasy animal hides over his growling belly, stumbled over a snow-packed hillside and gaped at meadows knee deep in grass. The anonymous explorer probably hollered to drive wolves away from a half-rotted elk carcass and gnawed it himself. Disputes in the valley are only slightly more sophisticated today.

Most people who see Jackson Hole want to move in. Half of them are rich, or expect to be, so they buy land and build a new house. Thousands of people love that area—and adore four-wheel drives, snowmobiles, hot tubs, flush toilets, maid service, and restaurants. Scientists study natural habitat at one end of the valley, while at the other bulldozers break ground for resorts so more people can enjoy the shrinking space and increasingly nervous wildlife. Many people who work to hold up the shiny facade—waiting tables, cleaning houses, building houses, packing groceries, shoveling snow, and piloting rafts—can't afford to live there. Some share old motels or tents, or drive over a high pass each day from towns in Idaho. Jackson may be interpreted as either an environmental nightmare or a diagram of the West's future.

Two weeks' lodging and food there would cost more than my workshops pay, so Jerry and I take a small camping trailer and our own food. While I'm not working, we investigate the Hole with Frodo's help.

One afternoon we drive up a rocky back trail where the pickup labors and thumps, leaning precariously. The road below looks like a thread when we park and hike along an angular shoulder below Sleeping Indian Mountain. Far below, an aspen grove shines vivid green on the mountain's dusty flank. Late wildflowers scent the air: Lavender Rocky Mountain iris and blue lupine stand above legions of pink geraniums; stonecrop and yellow violets button down the rocks. Cinquefoil blooms flutter like canaries above fading wild roses. We walk along the rim of a deep ravine angling toward the mountain and sit on a rock listening to ravens squawk. The valley is brimming with people, but at this height it is as quiet as it was two centuries ago. The Gros Ventre Indians—pronounced "grow vawnt"; the name means "big bellies"—must have lived abundantly in this valley now flatulent with human greed. On the horizon, the

Grand Teton flourishes a plume of snow. The human hordes are invisible.

By the time we climb back into the pickup, headed down to fish the Gros Ventre River, my bad knee is swollen and jerky with pain. I smashed it when I was about fourteen when my horse collided with another, and it has hurt more or less steadily ever since. Yesterday's hard ride was a strain. At the aspen grove, Jerry pulls over to cut walking sticks for us.

The incline approaching the trees is covered with tall, woody sage, but among the aspen the ground grows spongy, thick with saw-edged meadow grass. Shredded bark hangs on many of the trees, gnawed by elk confined here by last winter's deep snow. As I move through the tiny thicket, I half expect a bull elk to materialize, remembering an incident that convinced me elk can teleport like science fiction heroes.

———

I was hiking in the Black Hills late one autumn day nearly twenty years ago. No, really I was stumbling through a maze of narrow gulches braided around piles of rock in a forest. Sinking, the sun glowered as I blundered in what I hoped was the direction of my car, stashed in the underbrush along a road somewhere to the east. Hike straight toward it, I decided. Trust the inner compass.

Darkness slithered down valleys behind me as I scrambled up a ridge bristling with pines. Left and right I glimpsed asphalt, but my mutilated boots didn't know which way to turn. Either way, I needed to march while the light held, or I would stumble through the brush all night.

I reached a cluster of scrawny aspen scattered along the top of a limestone cliff. Shredded bark left from elk feeding in winter

decked the twisted trunks, stunted leaves trembled. Standing on tiptoe, I viewed the whole miniature grove, Ms. Gulliver in a lilliputian
forest. Sunlight fell on a bed-sized flat rock in a central clearing the
size of a suburban bedroom. I lay down and inhaled deeply, hoping
for fresh energy, warmth to stay with me in the next stony gulch.

This hike was research, since I was on the old trail of Lame
Johnny, a horse thief who lived in the Black Hills in the late 1800s.
I'd named the press for the bad man when Daniel and I started the
literary magazine at the ranch. Later I realized how little I knew
about the outlaw, yet some of my neighbors are grandchildren of the
vigilantes who hanged him from an elm tree. Asking questions
about the hanging is still considered indiscreet; in our part of the
West, "indiscreet" is college talk for "hazardous to your health."
Still, a woman had written to say that she'd once lived in the area
where I was hiking, and found hidden caves where the horse thief
hid herds until he could sell them. With a new set of topographical
maps, I began slipping away from ranch work to explore. Now I
realize I was trying to rebel against my father's strict schedule.
Quietly, I'd conformed to most of the rules of college and graduate
school. For seven years, I yielded to Daniel's peculiar beliefs about
marriage. But my habit of abiding a man's domination had begun to
disintegrate.

During that summer, I spent afternoons driving and hiking in
an area of the Black Hills so rough it was free of trash. My 1954
Chevy was high enough to clear most rocks, its three-thousand-
pound frame stable on winding tracks. After it sank hub deep in
mud, I walked through a herd of buffalo, practicing invisibility.
When I high-centered it on top of a mountain, I pried it loose with a
jack and a downed tree, knowing no one would come along to help.

On one hike earlier that summer, I'd found a cave in a box
canyon. Sitting down to rest on a ledge, I noticed a pile of fresh scat,

the rolls of waste as big around as my wrist and packed with chokecherry pits and acorns. I'm no feces expert, but the evidence convinced me that I was rested enough to hike somewhere else. Experts insist it's unlikely bears live in the Black Hills today, though Indians hunted grizzlies there before General George Custer's troops photographed their trophies and made the hides into coats. Surviving bears probably fell down mineshafts or were flattened by logging trucks or tourist campers. Walking among those hidden hollows that summer, I earned the smile I wear when some pompous expert *guaran-damn-tees* that no bears live in the Hills.

When I lay down on the flat rock in the clearing, I hadn't forgotten about bears, but I was sure I'd hear any animal that approached through the scrawny aspens. In the stillness after my clumsy human steps, the aspen leaves clicked, crows cawed. Twenty breaths, I promised, before I moved. Trucks ground gears on a highway thirty miles away. My muscles relaxed.

As I took the nineteenth breath, nearly asleep, the aspens hissed and snapped as a large body shoved them aside. I stopped breathing.

The aspens hissed again, leaves crunching under a heavy foot. Tiny hairs all over my body swiveled toward the sound. My eyes snapped open.

A bull elk stood just inside the clearing, staring at me, head up. His brown eyes flickered with furious red light. Body heat blasted me. He was ready for mating season, the annual fall rut. His muscles were sheathed in fat, his tawny hair iridescent with health. On his thick neck, the dark brown mane trembled. His antlers spread wider than his chestnut body, wider than my arms could reach. The massive coronet loomed over a broad brow, sweeping over his head, back and up like tree branches. He honed and polished those horns on trees, probably in this private grove. Uninvited, I lay in the dressing room of a dedicated warrior.

All the elk lore in my brain dwindled to one question: Had an elk ever killed a human during the rut?

The points of his horns flashed as he tipped his head forward to inspect me. The words of an erudite friend flashed through my brain: "Them sonsabitches are meaner than dirt even without hardons. You need a hand-held rocket to go traipsing after a full-growed elk."

The bull snorted, massive chest expanding, mane shivering until it filled my vision. With one smashing sound, he turned and leapt into the aspens.

His abrupt disappearance was impossible. He couldn't maneuver that massive rack of antlers among the tree trunks without making a sound. I should see trees thrashing and quivering as he battered a way through. I stood on tiptoe, high enough on my platform to see fifty feet into the surrounding pines. Nothing. Aspen leaves on the edges of the clearing shuddered in a light sunset breeze.

I lurched through the aspens, flailing against the branches. Stepping into thick pine darkness, I realized he might simply have stopped. I tiptoed in a circle, staring hard, trying to see his shape among the trees. Trotting down the ridge, I stopped every ten wobbly steps to listen, sure I would hear him. Not a sound.

I shake my head to pull my thoughts back to modern Jackson Hole and away from that meeting twenty years ago in the Black Hills. It occurs to me that I'd better do a little more research on elk, since a herd was sighted last week only three miles from the ranch. Experts are delighted that the animals seem to be reclaiming their ancient prairie range but are worried about the reason: Development in the Black Hills is forcing them down out of the trees. During the whole history of ranching in our area, elk have been absent from their old habitat, and we ranchers will face quite a challenge if we must learn how to deal with them as a part of our natural surroundings.

Ahead of me, Jerry walks confidently into the aspen grove to search for walking sticks. The first twisted tree we choose retains a few green leaves but stands so nearly naked of bark it cannot survive. "Elk chewed the bark off," Jerry says, using his knife to begin cutting it free of the ground.

As Jerry moves deeper among the trees, I tiptoe behind him, watching alertly. I've never been closer to an elk than I was that day in the aspens. When the elk returns in my dreams, I memorize details I missed seeing in his live appearance. Some nights I still wake dazed by his power, afraid to meet him in the flesh.

A thin wail near my ear makes me see a gray bird the size of my thumb on the top of a single young pine. As I take one more step, the bird flies to an aspen, screeching at the dangerous predator it hopes to lure away from its nest. Since I'm a sneaky human predator, I look closely at the pine instead. Slowly I circle the tree, peering at eye level between the branches without touching them, until I see a woven bundle of brown swamp grasses supported by twigs. Branches form its roof and prevent passing animals from knocking it free. The inner cup is no larger than my two thumbs, lined with white hair that might be from an elk, a horse, or a cow. Inside lie two minute eggs of a rich blue-green spattered with deep brown. The adult bird—perhaps a pine siskin—cheeps once more and flies away. I hope I have not caused her to abandon her nest.

Jerry tosses our sticks in the back of the pickup and drives along the Gros Ventre until we find a faint track leading down to the water. We park beside the river below a small lake. Jerry grabs his fishing rod and moves off through thick willows. The only way to keep the line from tangling at every step is to raise the pole over-head, and I trace his progress by that bobbing vertical line.

For a few minutes, I simply stand by the pickup flexing my inflamed knee, drinking from the water jug. I tie twenty feet of nylon rope on Frodo's leather collar. He hates being leashed after running wild on the ranch, but if he chases a rabbit in this thick brush, he might get lost. He also has a long history of jumping into running water too deep for his short legs. I pick up the walking stick and weave a path through the willows to the river.

Cautiously, I climb up a broad rock beside the rapids, well back from the edge. Here, only a few miles from its headwater trickle, the Gros Ventre is a brawling, surging mountain stream squashed into a narrow gorge that's more rock than liquid. I tie Frodo's rope around my ankle and watch while he begins his personal exploration before laying claim to the neighborhood. While he is scratching at a hollow beneath a pile of debris, I open the jackknife George gave me, still sharp from his last honing. Amazing. He's been dead nearly five years, and the knife he sharpened for me still holds its edge.

I hold the walking stick up so the sun catches it and study the native artwork left by a hungry elk gnawing its signature. Easily, the knife blade cuts through the remaining green bark, slipping under broad strips, lifting them to drop into the river. The wood beneath is glazed and glossy, almost transparent. Lying across my lap and hands, the stick is dense with vitality, smelling of thin mountain soil and snowmelt. Elk killed this tree and others by girdling them, stripping too much bark. Old cicatrices show that the tree once survived this damage, but the elk ate too much, or were too numerous. Around the white core, the wood is mottled in shades of brown and tan like a fawn's disguise. I pare only the top layer from those old scars. Finished, the stick's natural motif will resemble the spots on an Appaloosa horse.

Between strokes I watch the glassy green surface of the river, foaming white among the rocks and stranded logs. I see Jerry disappear around a downstream bend and continue to stare at the water, hypnotized by the current, remembering how peaceful George's face looked as he fished. Jerry has suffered through the past three months of turmoil with me, listening as I've endlessly debated my obligations to my parents, waiting up for me when I drive back from the ranch late at night. He needs a break.

Across the river, a motion draws my eye: a horse's tail switching flies. Through thick brush I glimpse a horse's head, a brown-coated rider. Several on horseback follow the track we drove down. No sound carries over the river's chatter. Dizzy from watching the current, I'm not sure if the riders are passing as I watch, or if I see century-old ghosts: mountain men slipping into the valley to hunt. Their somber clothes, nearly invisible in the dark trees, give the lie to their own existence. The sight makes me smile, thinking how George half-believed in time travel. When we loaded the van to head for a summer of camping, he always hoped we'd be transported back to 1840 with all our gear.

My arm and hand fall into a satisfying rhythm: cut, lift, slide. As the stick's weight molds to my hands, my fingers seek rough spots without guidance from my eyes.

A pinching at the ankle of my knee-high moccasin makes me look for Frodo. He's dragged the rope around a willow branch and strains against his collar, nosing a snake hole. I put down my knife and stick to untangle the rope from his back leg and assorted branches. He leans against my leg, panting as he inspects the river.

Whittling, I stare at the mountain behind me before I realize what I am seeing. A broad face of bare rock hangs above a wooded slope pocked with boulders—the wound left by the Gros Ventre slide of 1925. That three-minute earthquake transformed the land-

scape, slamming a huge chunk of mountain into the valley. As
Seldom Seen Smith said in *The Monkey Wrench Gang,* "All we need
here, God, is one little precision earthquake" to solve the crowding
problems in Jackson Hole and cut through a lot of pointless blather.

Most of the trees growing on slopes that moved survived the
trip. Plants native to higher elevations now live on the slopes below.
We often regard trees as symbols of wisdom or endurance, oracles of
a single site. Like mountains, they seem to meditate in one place,
without travel to broaden outlook and insight. Their constancy leads
us to think of them as dependable, but, plainly, trees are not as fixed
as we might suppose. Those above me traveled with the soil, dam-
aged roots perhaps slowing their growth for a season or two. The
rock above them was swept bare by the slide, and no doubt some
trees were crushed. But it's nearly impossible to tell which migrated
and which did not.

Staring at the trees, I think of my father, devoting his life to a
few thousand acres of prairie. Like most ranchers, once he chose to
become a rancher, he was consistent, an admirable trait. But now it's
time for him to slow down, to allow me to set the terms of my own
pledge to the ranch. I know he's sick in body and mind. I think he
knows it. I've worn the road thin between Cheyenne and the ranch
racing back and forth this summer. Perhaps I have no choice now
but to leave my folks alone to find their own fate.

The rope tightens on my ankle again. Upstream, Frodo stands
among rocks in shallow water, looking toward willows quaking as a
fisherman struggles through them. On his short legs, the dog is solid
as a monument, broad back expressing stability, tail vibrating with
enthusiasm. Just watching him makes me smile.

Perched on a warm rock beside the river, below the vast lacera-
tion of the slide, I peel the walking stick, thinking how such a staff
offers balance, a brace against falls. My father's teaching was my

childhood groundwork, offering perspective as I followed Daniel into disaster. Following George, evasive and enigmatic as an elk, guided me to this time and place. Now what? I live with Jerry, but since my father has turned on me like a wounded elk, how can I trust another man?

Frodo eyes the tumbling water. Then he stiffens, and his ears rise as he wades into the current. Twice his feet slip on rocks as he watches the brush across the river.

He is staring at the spot where I saw the riders a few minutes ago. Does he think George is among them? "No, Frodo," I say, "You can't follow George. I need you alive." I'm tempted to tell the dog about my dream of the box of bones, to explain that George used the dream to remind me that he is truly gone. I think he was saying a final good-bye, confident that I can now live best without him. I call to Frodo, hoping that he will not be foolish enough to jump into the stream. I'm still holding my knife and the walking stick.

He glances once over his shoulder at me, then lunges into the seething current. I scramble awkwardly up, my legs numb from sitting. I try to call him again, but no sound comes from my throat. For a moment, his short legs paddle vigorously before the river lifts him and rolls him under. When his head breaks water, he coughs and sinks under the green waves. The rope cuts into my ankle.

I hurl the stick and knife backward and grab the rope. The water's force jerks me down to a sitting position on the rock. Taut, the rope disappears in the center of the stream. I brace myself and pull, the line burning my hands, trying to remember what kind of knot I tied to Frodo's collar. If it slips, he'll be swept out of reach. If it's a bowline, perhaps I can pull him out. Or perhaps the river will take me too.

Braced, I step into the water. Cold fills my moccasins, and I stumble, trying to stand against the stream's thrust. I haul back on the rope until Frodo's head pops out of the water. He is paddling hard and snorting. Hand over hand, I draw him through the heaving water until I can reach under his belly. When I straighten, holding him against my chest, I sag with his weight. Staggering, I throw him to the rock. He scrambles to the center and shakes himself while I babble his name and lurch to shore.

I wrap my jacket around him, looking for Jerry. Across the river, he plays his line, intently watching the spot where it enters the water. Picking up my knife and walking stick, I hustle through rocks and tangled willows to the pickup. I start the engine and turn the heat high. Holding Frodo on my lap, I pull a blanket from behind the seat and drape it over both of us. Frodo's compact body shivers, plucking my nerves until I am shuddering. Sobbing, I feel the dog's comforting bulk slump into me. Our hearts pulse and our blood heat blends until I no longer know which of us is warmer, or colder.

When the well of tears within me is as empty as on the day I shot the sick steer, when I can see again, the trees below the earthquake scar throw long shadows. The lake above the river is still, reflecting a gold sky as Jerry walks steadily toward us beside the river. He opens the pickup door and looks in, his expression changing as he reads the story in the damp spots, the shivering dog, and my tears. He drops his pole, slides inside and wraps his arms around me and my dog, holding us safe.

Climbing into
the Bull Pen

*Far out on the Wyoming plains, I was still a hundred miles from the
ranch on a hot July day when I first saw the haze—a dirty brown cloud
hovering above the pale blue mounds of the Black Hills.*

*All my life, I have looked to the Hills for clues about the immediate
future. A thunderstorm that veered around the south side of the peaks, for
example, would usually hit our ranch, while clouds that moved north-
ward would miss us. Black or purple clouds bubbling up meant a fire in
the nearby forests, while a purple haze signaled fires burning in the
Rocky Mountains. The brown haze looked like the dust we usually see
rising from the plains on a windy spring day when someone plows native
grasses that should never be turned over. I soon realized that this particular darkness was pollen from the pine trees and from the plains grasses
knee-deep after heavy spring rains.*

*Grasses I hadn't seen for years waved alongside my car as I drove
down the ranch road: timothy and orchard grass, porcupine and witch
grass. Native prairie plants, adapted by centuries of life here to variable
weather, had taken advantage of the humidity to spread. Each surly
breeze swept pollen into the murky air.*

*I recalled how difficult breathing was in past years with high pollen
counts. Cows coughed all night, and Frodo wheezed in rhythm with*

George's labored breathing. My sinuses became so infected I was reminded of a day on the beach at Galveston, Texas, when someone held a shell against my ear and said, "Listen! It's the ocean!" In this "sea of grass" I once heard the ocean in my right ear for a month.

I parked the car in front of my garage and surveyed shades of green flowing everywhere around Windbreak House. The colors were impossible to describe because I'd never seen such a mixture before. Around me, an intricate tapestry of prairie life prospered as if highways and houses did not exist. For twenty seasons of meager moisture, life here had withered. Now it flourished.

Before going inside, I walked among my trees. By the time I returned to the house, my ankle-length skirt was shimmering with new gold threads: seeds from cheat grass and porcupine grass, called devil's needle. I stepped out of the skirt and shook it hard. A few of the tenacious pests fell and were swept into a stand of wildflowers, where they would sprout next spring. So I got a wastebasket and sat in shade beside Frodo, already tired from exploring the woodpile. One by one I detached the seeds and deposited them carefully in the basket so I could burn them in the trash barrel, protecting this earth from invasion. Futile. Grass seeds could wait throughout my lifetime and a dozen more for another chance at life.

I was still opening windows and turning on fans to air out my house when my father knocked on the door. He'd walked to my house to ask me if I would take a picture of the field east of his house. "I've never seen the brome grass this tall," he said. "Not in eighty years."

He rode with me to the alfalfa field and told me the picture should show that the brome grass was taller than the Bronco. He refused to stand beside the car—he hated having his picture taken. In eighty years, he had posed for only two studio pictures: one when he graduated from high school and another when he and my mother were married. Once or twice I wrapped a camera in a jacket and smuggled it along when we *worked in the corral or pastures, so I could steal a few shots when he wasn't looking.*

While I focused on the grass, he stood beside me. His shadow fell across the field, stretching to the base of the high ridge to the south and dwindling into the pastures beyond. He always said, "My shadow on this place is worth ten bucks a day." In the picture, at least, his silhouette will always lie across this land.

The crash of the whole solar and stellar systems could only kill you once.

—THOMAS CARLYLE

I call Mother as soon as we return to Cheyenne and learn that she and my father went to the Mayo Clinic in Minnesota while Jerry and I were in Jackson. She says their doctors pronounced both of them to be in perfect health, and she's already looking forward to their winter vacation in Texas, which reminds her to tell me I'd better move back home pretty soon so I can water her plants and feed her cats during the winter.

How did they manage the long drive to and from the clinic? I ask. Oh, she says, Father just pulled over for a nap whenever he felt dizzy or tired. They found a couple of motels that weren't too expensive. "You know I always take my hot pot so I can fix our soup for supper," she adds. My father refuses to come to the telephone.

For the next three days, I tell myself that I am resting from the workshop as I answer mail, tidy the house, and add the figures in my checkbook over and over. I take particular care with every task, reluctant to go to the ranch. My savings account is nearly empty. Soon I will have to decide whether to work for my father or get a job in Cheyenne. I write each morning, reliving on paper every argument with my parents during the past ten years, becoming convinced that their downward spiral began long ago. I can imagine no happy ending, nor decide upon any action of mine that will help them.

This morning I wake before dawn, my head heavy with premonition. When the sun begins to rise, heat spills over the horizon and surges through the city streets in waves I can almost see. In a light dress and sandals I head for the ranch before the morning rush.

Filling the car with gas, I think of the long drive ahead. Now that I am beginning to believe I can create a new life with Jerry in Cheyenne, why do I return to the ranch so often? Most people my age are so immersed in their own lives they have little contact with their parents until the old folks get sick enough to warrant nursing home care. On each trip back, I become engrossed in the unfinished work I notice around the ranch. My mind fills with the details of my parents' lives and problems, and I find it difficult to return to Cheyenne.

I glide into a space between speeding trucks on the interstate, listening to old tapes and hardly seeing the rugged cliffs and green grass. While Jim Croce sings that sometimes you eat the bear and "sometimes the bear eats you," I can feel the grizzly's rotten breath on my face. Every few minutes I realize my hands hurt because they are clenched on the steering wheel. My jaw is rigid with tension. I remind myself to relax, straightening my back until I hear neck bones popping.

Every time I head north from Cheyenne, my head begins to throb and my skull thumps with migraine pain. Somewhere along the narrow highway, I find a driveway, pull over beside tall sagebrush, and get out, holding on to the fender while I throw up everything I have eaten that morning. Pure fear, I tell myself. I'm terrified of my parents' deterioration. Back in the car, I fasten my seat belt and admit another fear: that as my parents decline, I will lose any chance to return to the ranch, even as a visitor. That I will never again watch the sun rise out of the Badlands to gild the buffalo grass around my own house.

My father's attitude toward me shows no signs of improvement. Tonight I'll take the next step on my expressway to city life: I will call the couple who wants to rent my ranch house and tell them they can move in next week. As this day has approached, I have sorted through everything in my house, remnants of my life there with George, hauling loads of discards to the Salvation Army and the Rapid City dump. On each return trip to Cheyenne, I have packed my car with reference books and photograph albums. Since I don't want to fill the house I share with Jerry with reminders of George, I've stowed some things in a single room in the basement of my ranch house that the renters will not need. My high school annuals, and George's, are stacked on a basement shelf with our wedding pictures, the photo albums he made before we met, our love letters, and other souvenirs. I tucked the curls George's mother and mine saved from our first haircuts into a trunk with some of his clothes. Anything I can't pack into my car tonight, I'll cram into the basement room before I lock the door.

I hear my father's ultimatum in every revolution of the car's tires. How could he give me such an impossible choice—to give up writing and help him, or to get out and not come back? Does he even remember saying it? For years I've juggled ranch work with writing and teaching to earn enough money to live. My father was often angry when I left, but George could sometimes intervene, deflect the fury.

Over and over during the years George and I lived on the ranch, and while I lived there as a widow, my friends asked, "What if you had to choose the ranch or writing?"

I'd shake my head. Impossible. My father never approved of my writing, but he always encouraged me to work for what I wanted. I worked hard on the ranch, and he knew I wanted to stay. I had been sure he'd manage some compromise. Now I wonder if I've been wrong.

"Will you own it when he dies?" my friends have asked. I've always answered with a shrug. "I'm an only child. Who else?" But I don't know the terms of his will or what he might do to change it now that he seems convinced I am his enemy.

When I first fled to Cheyenne, I expected Jerry to be as unreliable as the other men in my life, so I'd have to go back to the ranch. At other times, I told myself I'd simply return to the ranch if my father died, or offered me a partnership. When someone asked for my Cheyenne address and telephone number, I said I was "staying with a friend." In the months since my move, I haven't worked on a poem, but I love Jerry and our life together. Now that I've chosen writing over ranching, what will happen to me if I can't write? What will I do if my father sells the ranch? If he dies and leaves it to my mother and she sells it? Or marries again?

Only in my journal do I admit how much I enjoy writing with the study door shut in Cheyenne so I can't hear the telephone. I savor impulsive midday trips to a grocery store six blocks away, pleased that I don't have to ask my parents what they need from town or survey the pantry to calculate two weeks' meals before I shop. This city living, I've confided to my journal, has some benefits.

I've returned to the ranch nearly every weekend since moving to Cheyenne. My father is easier to get along with if I go to my parents' house early in the morning and sit in my old place at the breakfast table. Then he behaves as if I am a child again, and I trot dutifully after him as he goes out to his daily chores.

Yet each time we drive the pastures, he asks me questions he might ask a ranch manager, not a child. Where are the bulls? Why did I put cows into a pasture we never use in summer? If I remind him that I've been in Cheyenne and he must have moved the cattle when I wasn't here, he says, "Your job is to be with me as long as it's daylight."

Recently, as I left the ranch, he remarked that he'd asked a buyer to look at the cattle. I suggested, not for the first time, that he hire help, naming several reliable neighborhood men. He walked away without a word. Five days later, when I returned, he told me to buy a bull or two to breed the two-year-old heifers. I thought he might be thinking more clearly, giving me a competency test. I located a pair of good young Angus bulls at a nearby ranch. My father hadn't offered me a check as he once did when I bought ranch supplies, so I paid for the bulls and for delivery. The next weekend, he raged at me, contradicting himself with nearly every sentence. Why did I buy bulls since he's selling the ranch? Now that I've abandoned him, how can he handle spring calving by himself?

Before my parents returned from last winter's stay in Texas, he told me to buy a new Ford pickup. "You've always bought Chevys," I pointed out. "Get a Ford," he snapped. But when he got home, he was furious. "What would I want with a Ford?" he said. The next time I came home, my 1985 Ford pickup was not in my locked garage. He'd managed to trade it and the new Ford for a Chevrolet pickup—without having me sign a bill of sale or the title.

Now each Saturday when we tour the pastures, he complains about the new pickup. Everything about it, from its blinking lights to its door latches, confuses him. One day he drove off alone, set the emergency brake, then drove three miles to my house and asked me how to release it. I showed him the instruction book in the glove compartment, but he said furiously—this man who once read a dozen magazines and a couple of books a week—that he doesn't have time to read that damn nonsense. As we look over the cows, he drives and counts them over and over, forgetting the totals. I scribble the numbers in my own notebook when he's not looking.

Several times a day, he has what he calls a dizzy spell and goes inside for a nap. I furtively load into his pickup the supplies he'll need for the next week, posts and sacks of feed he can no longer lift. In the evenings, I call my uncle Harold to tell him how my father is behaving and ask his advice. He, too, seems helpless. "I hardly know your paw anymore," he says. "He's not the man he was."

———

My car tops the last hill before the ranch drive. By reflex I glance east. I'm always relieved, almost surprised, to see my house still standing, with my parents' house and the corrals beyond it. Since I didn't take time to shop for food this morning, and my refrigerator and cupboards are empty, I will visit the little café in Hermosa this evening to eat and listen to neighbors talk. I store up what they say about my parents' behavior as if enough information will create a solution.

My mother is rattling pans in the kitchen when I knock. She shrieks, startled, and comes to the door drying her hands on a towel. When she sees me, she wails as she does every Friday evening, "Oh! You're home! I've been so worried. You didn't tell me where you were going, or how long you'd be gone."

Again I show her my Wyoming address and phone number on the cover of her phone book. She laughs and says it's time I quit fooling around. Lowering her voice, she confides that maybe

Father's memory is slipping a little. He asked the name of their insurance agent. "But you know," she says, "you should come home. Your father's always right."

I suggest again that they both see a local doctor and remind her of the information I gave her about strokes and Alzheimer's disease—still in a pile of unopened mail on the dining room table. I make instant coffee for both of us and try to get her to sit down and talk.

Near sunset, I put my coffee cup in the sink and head for the door to go to my dark house on the hill. My father hasn't come home yet. "He stays out awfully late these days," Mother says. "Without you here to help, he has so much more work to do. You know, Father's Day is this month. Why don't you come back where you belong for your present?"

Impatient with her repetitions, I turn to leave. "What is your phone number up at that house?" Mother asks. "You never told me."

"Don't you remember?" I say. "George and I lived there for ten years before he died. You dialed that number a dozen times a day— see, it's still on your blackboard."

"But now all I ever get is your answering service, and that woman is driving me crazy." Her eyes fill with tears. "She won't tell me anything. I call every day, hoping you've come home."

"Mother, that's my voice. It's a tape-recorded message. I don't answer the phone because I live in Wyoming. See, here's my phone number in Cheyenne, on the cover of the phone book."

Just then my father jerks open the screen door. "Well, it's my daughter," he says, drawing the words out. "When did you decide to drop by? Going to stay overnight this time, or are you just on your way to New York City to be a famous writer?" His lips tighten. "Get out here and help me."

I follow like a robot. He's always warned me to change clothes if the job is likely to be messy or take long, so I assume he wants me for something simple like holding a wrench. I follow him to the corral, lit by the spotlight on the barn. An angry bellow blasts the air, startling me so much I trip over a broken post. Split planks lie scattered among crowbars and hammers. A fence has been built across the corner of a large corral. Inside the little triangular pen stands a huge Angus bull, his blunt head raised and nostrils flaring red.

My father kneels among coils of wire and metal fence panels, frowning. "I've been trying to keep this bull in, and I can't seem to get the electric fence to work right," he says.

Puzzled, I squat down beside the batteries. Electricity has never been one of my better subjects. When I was a child, Father tested his fence hookups by having me hold both ends. If I jumped at the slight current as he flipped the switch, he knew it worked. No matter how many times he shocked me, I always dutifully grabbed the wire. Still, I've learned enough about electricity to say, "Your connections are reversed. This one's positive."

"I've tried it that way. It doesn't work," he snaps.

Thinking, I look up at the bull and realize I don't recognize him. "Isn't this a new bull?"

"Yes. I got him last week at the sale, but he's torn down half the corrals. I'll teach him to stay in, or kill him," Father says, panting.

I look around the corral. Tangled wire is wrapped around posts and planks nailed higher than my head. Nails stick out in all directions. "Why don't you just turn him out with the other bulls?"

"Because I want him with my cows, that's why. That's how we get calves on a ranch."

"You've never turned bulls with the cows this late in the summer."

"Well, I'm doing it now. I had too many dry cows. You'd know that if you were ever around."

"But they'll calve in the middle of the summer!"

"Why don't you stop telling me how to run my ranch and shut your mouth and give me a hand with this electric fence? Another week short of feed and water, maybe he'll settle down and behave the way I want him to."

We spend an hour making the same connections over and over. My father's speech rambles, as if vital links in his brain have been unplugged. The bull spins in the small space, eyes rolling back in his head, foam dripping from his jaws. Half a fifty-gallon barrel we use to water confined animals lies on its side in his pen, and the feed trough is empty. The bull's sides look gaunt.

When I reach for a hammer and tear my dress on the fence, my father says, "What are you doing out here dressed like that? Go home and put on some clothes. And hurry up. I want to finish this tonight."

Long after dark, he announces that the batteries are too rusty to work. "I'll go to town tomorrow and get more. You get some supper and get to bed. That is, if you're not gadding around somewhere else."

When I go inside my house, the door bangs back against the wall with a hollow sound in the nearly empty space. I throw my suitcase in the bedroom and fix a sandwich, then call my mother to ask about the new bull. She says Father came back from the sale ring with the animal last week. He shut the bull into the main corral, saying he'd turn him out with the cows right away. By the next day the new bull was in a neighbor's pasture. So my father, who hadn't been on a horse since he sold Zarro twenty years ago, saddled my young Arab gelding, Oliver, and rode into the pasture. When he came back with the bull, Mother says, the horse was lathered and throwing his head. Father tied him to a corral post and beat him with a stock whip until, he told her, he couldn't raise his arm anymore. Then he shut the horse in a small corral next to the barn. It's time, he said, that horse learned who was boss. Linda spoiled him.

Next I call Uncle Harold, who says my dad hasn't done a thing but fight with the bull all week. "I don't know what's wrong with your dad. His fences are falling down, but he spends all day in the corral with that damn bull. I had no idea he'd let the place go like it has. I told my man to slip through his pastures a couple times this week to see the cows aren't short of water." His hearing aid whines into the receiver.

"He's sick, Harold. He's been having strokes—Mother said his face was pulled down on one side most of last winter. He can't remember anyone's name. Could you talk him into seeing a doctor?"

"Linda, he's just being stubborn, like he's been all his life. Has to do things his way. I saw him chasing that bull. Thought at first it was some kid like you." He snorts. "Runnin' back and forth on that hillside all afternoon. I thought he was gonna kill the horse and the bull both." He sighs. "Then the next day, he called that new neighbor—what's his name?—to help him move a few cows across the railroad tracks. I saw them over there, guy was using your saddle and that gray horse of yours. But the cows are all mixed up. He's got unbranded calves in there and cows that'll calve in a month. Can't take those to summer pasture." Eventually, Harold stops fuming and hangs up. I realize he will do nothing.

I step outside and sit in a chair on the deck to think. The darkness folds over me. I sit for a long time listening to the quiet sounds around me: a frog at the pond, the whoosh of a nighthawk catching a mosquito. Then the bull bawls from the corral below.

From the deck I look down at the lighted kitchen window in my parents' house. I know Mother is still in the kitchen, washing the bowls she used to serve the same soup she has served every single night for forty years. The first time she fixed the tomato, celery, and

rice concoction, my father said he liked it, so she's never fixed anything else. How can they stand it? Light from the kitchen window
casts deep shadows among the pine trees my father planted around
the new house the year he brought us to the ranch.

———————

Since I was nine years old, every road I've traveled has ended here
on the ranch. I have immersed myself in learning the lessons of this
particular piece of ground and remained here, faithful to my bond,
even after George died. I have pledged myself in blood to this land,
this buffalo grass, placing my connection with my father and his
land—the two are inseparable—above every other consideration. I
think my intense need to write made me miss seeing how ill George
was until it was too late. But my writing has occupied only the
cracks and pauses in my life compared to the time and space occupied by the ranch. Now that I have taken the first step away, I'd better keep going.

My father, the man who raised me, is gone. I'm dealing with an
irrational stranger. It's time to stop trying to pay what I owe him for
raising me. Perhaps when I called myself a survivor, hunkering tight
into this sod, I was only afraid. Now I've tasted the dust of another
place, and I can learn new languages from odors on the wind.
Finally, I must travel a road that leads me away from the ranch.

Back in the house, I call the couple who wants to rent my house,
and we arrange that they will move in next week. I try again to
explain that my parents may not behave rationally, and they assure
me that they will be patient and let me know anything important.

The next morning I help my father add planks until the corral
fence stands nearly ten feet high. He doesn't mention getting more
batteries for the electric fence. Every move we make provokes the

bull to snort and pace his prison. His hide grows dark with sweat. His nose drips blood, and his head is covered with scabs.

When we stop for lunch, I walk behind the barn and find Oliver tied to a stout post in a small round corral. He is rawboned and scrawny. I'm leading him to the water tank when my father yells, "You leave that horse right there. I want him to quiet down so I can handle him. He damn near killed me."

"He won't get any quieter without water," I say, and keep going.

Father follows, carrying his whip. When he gets close, the horse rolls his eyes and shies, then tries to jerk away, lifting me off my feet. "See?" Father says. "He's jumpy around that whip. I want him to get used to it."

"He's fifteen years old," I say. "He's always hated the whip, so I don't think you're going to change his mind now." For a moment I think my father will strike me, but he walks away. At the tank, the gelding buries his nose in water and gulps frantically while I scratch his neck. Several cuts on his head are scabbed over, and his ribs are scraped raw in patches. He rolls his eyes back as he drinks, twitching his ears to hear if something is sneaking up on him.

That afternoon, we work again on the corral. "Build a fence right," Father has always said, but he drags half-rotten planks out of the weeds and wires them up until the fence is a tangled mass of jagged boards and barbed wire.

Then he drops the crowbar in the bull's pen. "Get in there and get it," he says. In the tiny space, the bull throws his head up and bawls.

I glance at my father to see if he is joking. "No. How could you ask me to do that?"

"Get in there right now, or I will," he says, waving his hammer at me.

"Why don't we just call a trucker and get rid of him?" Father is going into the barn and doesn't hear me. I lie down and slide a tamping bar under the bottom plank to hook the crowbar. When I pull it toward me, the bull slams his head against the fence, driving a long splinter into my arm. He backs off, shaking his head. I yank the crowbar through and roll away. The bull lowers his head to stare at me between the planks, then lurches backward, squalling. When I stand up, he spins on his back legs and charges again, then recoils, staggering. If we turn him out in the pasture, he might kill the next person he meets.

When Father comes out of the barn, I hand him the crowbar and yank the splinter out of my bleeding arm. "Haven't you always said there's no point in trying to force cattle? You always said not to take risks—that somebody always gets hurt and it's not the cow."

"By God," he says, "if that bull doesn't do what I want him to, I'll kill him." He shakes his head. "I'm feeling a little dizzy in this heat. I'm going inside and lay down awhile." His eyes are bloodshot and the left side of his cheek sags, pulling his mouth toward his chin.

"You've had another stroke. Come on, let's get you to a doctor."

He faces me. "Did you go to medical school while you were running around the country? Don't try to tell me there's something wrong with me." He stomps toward the house.

That night, Uncle Harold calls to ask if the bull is still in the corral. He refuses to talk to my father about seeing a doctor. "Don't be surprised if I find a way to take care of that bull situation," he says as he hangs up.

The house is stuffy and the night unusually warm. I work hard, loading the car with the things I will take to Cheyenne and shoving the rest into the back of the basement. By the time I finish, I'm drenched with sweat and too tired to shower. I roll my sleeping pad out on the deck and try to pretend I've run away to the mountains. Long after midnight, a faint breeze blows across my face. Dozing, I hear the bull's moaning bellows from the corral below. Once in a while, wood splinters.

The next day, I walk into the yard just as my father is getting his pickup out of the garage. He tells me to saddle the horse and doesn't mention the bull. We spend the day checking fences close to home, working in silence that is almost companionable. He hauls fencing supplies while I ride Oliver up steep hills and into gullies to check and repair spots where Father won't take the pickup. At dark, he declares the day over and heads for home, leaving me to follow slowly on the horse. As I cross the last alfalfa field before the ranch buildings, I hear geese overhead and realize I don't hear the bull. Passing the corral, I see the pen is empty.

I ride Oliver up to my house and turn him into a little field below my house where he can graze, drinking from a small dam. I hang the saddle in a dark corner of the basement and throw a blanket over it so my father is unlikely to find it. Knowing someone else has used my saddle and horse makes me feel as if someone had borrowed my underwear.

As soon as I step inside, the phone rings. Uncle Harold tells me he saw us in the pasture and guessed we'd be busy all day so he sent two hired men to our place, one on horseback and the other with a truck and trailer. The bull knocked the horse and rider halfway across the corral while they were trying to load him. "Good men, though," he chuckles. "Just made 'em mad." They roped the bull and dragged him into the trailer. "Loaded the horse too, in case the bull busted out on the highway. Said by god if he got out, they'd chase him clear to the sale ring if they had to. One watched through the rear window while the other drove. Said the bull'd squat down on his haunches, then lunge and hit the front of the trailer. They didn't even slow down, afraid he'd land in their laps. Every time they came to a stop sign, they slammed on the brakes so hard so he fell down. Then they drove like hell until he got up and started banging around again. I'm not sure the horse will ever get over that ride. When they let the bull out at the sale ring, he put six men up on the fence."

Again I ask Harold to try talking my father into seeing a doctor. "He'd listen to you," I plead.

"Don't you worry about your paw," he says. "He's just having one of his fits. He always did that if he didn't get his way when we was kids. He'll get over it. I think he's getting meaner, though." Later that evening, Mother calls. She says Harold's just telephoned my father to say one of his bulls broke a leg. He needed a bull fast, he said, so he took ours and put a check in the mail.

"That bull wasn't for sale," Father yelled. "I was teaching him a lesson. By God, I'm going to ride over there in the morning and get him." No you won't, Harold said; he'd trucked the bull to his river ranch eighty miles away. My father hung up on him.

The next morning I lock my house, leaving a hidden key for the renters, and join my parents for breakfast. My father, who never raised his voice when I was growing up, yells, "Harold always had his way when we were kids!" He slams his fist on the table, spilling coffee. "Anything he wanted, he was big enough and strong enough to just take it. Never learned to do things any other way." He glares at me, spittle running from the corner of his mouth. His face is still twisted. He is a caricature of the kind man who sat in my mother's kitchen with his straw hat on his knee.

Nighthawks Fly in Thunderstorms

On a hot August day, I sat as usual before my computer trying to write an essay about nighthawks. I spent less time looking at the words on the screen than at the photograph propped on my desk, with my father's shadow stretching across the grass. All day I thought about my parents, and about the cattle scattered through our pastures.

Then, waiting for the computer to shut down, I recalled a dream I had a year or so before George died. As the dream began, I was sitting in my house at the ranch, sobbing. Someone I loved was dead. I couldn't remember who but thought it might be my father until he wrapped me in his sinewy arms, saying, "I promise that even though I leave you in the flesh, my spirit will be with you always."

The incongruities of the scene startled me awake. My father did not hug, apart from a few taut embraces when I was a child. If Mother kissed his cheek, he stiffened. He was not likely to quote the Bible, and he seldom went to church, though Mother had told me he'd begun reading the Old Testament after supper.

I sat up, fully awake, and looked out my bedroom window just in time to see his old pickup with no brakes or lights pull slowly onto the highway in front of a semi truck going eighty. The words he'd spoken in my dream were still clear in my mind. As the truck swerved, I leaped out of bed and pulled on my jeans, planning to race after him. Then I pictured myself saying he shouldn't drive that pickup on the highway, explaining that I'd dreamed he was dead. "You're just trying to get me off the highway," he'd say. "Anyway, what were you doing sleeping this late?"

At the time, I concluded that the dream emerged from the frustration George and I felt as we tried to get along with my father. We'd agreed by then that if the situation didn't improve, we would leave the ranch together to find a new life elsewhere. I'd admitted to George my fear of living anywhere but the ranch. What if I were trapped by indoor work? Guiltily, we both realized that if my father died, we could stay. It never crossed my mind that George might die first, leaving me trapped on the ranch with my father.

Looking at the recent photograph with the old dream freshly in mind, I thought of the history of grass. Seeds formed of this summer's heat and rain will wait through dry years to sprout, wait perhaps beyond the end of my lifetime. In some rainy season far in the future, ancient grasses will wake to cover these hills once more. People disappoint themselves and others. People die. But the genesis of grass is assured. I believe in the resurrection of the grass and its life everlasting.

I didn't go back to the ranch or talk to my father after he tried to send me into the bullpen in July. My mother called every Saturday morning to say over and over, "You know your father is right." I wanted to face my father, to say, "I AM your ranch." Looking at the picture, I realize that if I spoke to my father now, I would have to say, "I WAS your ranch, but you waited too long. You've lost me, and you will lose the ranch, and it's your own fault."

Behavior lawless as snow-flakes, words simple as grass.
—WALT WHITMAN
"Song of Myself"

Since I have stopped building each week around my Friday night trip to the ranch, I have begun to enjoy life in Cheyenne. I go to my computer soon after seven A.M. and write until noon, breaking my concentration only to prepare lunch. In the afternoon, I spend another hour or two writing before I get the mail and go to the grocery store.

Late each afternoon, I go to the small backyard behind the house to work in the garden, digging out dandelions, pulling weeds among the lettuce and radishes, and counting the grasshoppers caught in spider webs on the tomato plants. When Jerry comes home from work at five, we sit down with a beer until the air cools, then walk the dog in the park.

When I sit in the shade to enjoy the cooling breeze of the spinning sprinkler, Frodo comes to lay his head in my lap and sleep. I stroke the old dog's back and talk softly to him, but I believe he is so deaf he hardly hears me. This afternoon, as usual, I find myself listening for the boom of nighthawks. At the ranch, they spend summer evenings spiraling through the air over my hilltop house, snatching mosquitoes and millers. This city's sprawl lies on the same high plains terrain where I have spent so much of my life, so I sometimes see prairie animals among its pruned trees and lawns. One evening a kestrel cruised past. Walking Frodo in an empty field a few blocks away, I once heard a meadowlark. Redwing blackbirds nest in the cattails around the lake. In my journal, I record each tiny sign of prairie life, as if discovering treasures. And each night I scan the sunset sky over the refinery lights, searching for the familiar curved shape of a nighthawk's flight.

Tonight Jerry comes home so tired he doesn't bother to change clothes, just loosens his tie and sits in the shade. With two bottles of beer, I join him just as two friends stop by. As we visit, I point out six tomato plants heavy with green fruit. When they admire the rhubarb, I pull stalks for them and give them my pie recipe. I laugh at myself for practicing these customs of rural hospitality in the center of a city, but I am also proud of how much country I've tucked into our little square of green surrounded by pavement.

Over the low murmur of conversation, I hear a familiar *peenk-peenk*. My stomach rolls as I look up. Dozens of nighthawks wheel overhead, spinning and dipping. Most of the sky is empty, but our house is the center of a whirlwind. The familiar shapes rise and plunge, chase each other, execute barrel rolls in the air. The air hums with their flight. Tears pour down my face. I stand at the alley fence among the wildflowers to stare as the birds play, pulling so sharply out of dives they snap like bowstrings against the sunset. Crescent wind. I have never seen a nighthawk here before. Perhaps they are heading south for the winter, but why are so many of them together? Remembering what they have meant to me, I decide they are an omen, signifying an end to my questions about the future of the ranch and the direction of my life.

My first evening on the ranch, when I was nine years old, nighthawks plummeted like cannonballs into my life. My mother had just married John Hasselstrom, and I was helping her carry our suitcases and boxes to a tall house in the middle of a hay field. Its white paint weathered to gray, the old house had been lifted from the foundation where our new house would stand and deposited on railroad ties. We lived there all that summer of 1952, while the carpenters finished the new house near the garage and barn. When the wind blew hard behind a hailstorm, the house swayed like the cotton-woods beside it.

Knowing his instant family was used to lawns instead of hay, my father had hitched up the team of horses to mow the lanky alfalfa around the gray house the day before we arrived, raking it into fat windrows. The green hay was so heavy I tripped crossing it every time I carried a load of belongings into the house. Outside the trimmed rectangle, plants stood high as my armpits, shimmering in the breeze.

That first night, while Mother stayed in the house unpacking and cooking supper, I sat on the railroad-tie steps and watched my new father drive through the dense green in his pickup. I went down the steps to meet him and we stood together enjoying the sun-set, a ritual he has practiced all his life. Hundreds of birds dipped and swooped over my head, dark crescents against the sunset's gold. When I asked about the explosive sounds from the birds, he told me they were nighthawks.

At that moment, nighthawks became my favorite prairie bird. Even then, I knew the Lakota called them thunderbirds, but how I knew remains a mystery to me. The name's metaphor explained itself during the first thunderstorm I watched with my father, a tra-dition we began a few weeks later that summer.

Once we settled into the routine of ranch life, haying took up most of every day in August. The fields were often baked by the sun and bludgeoned by savage thunderstorms, hail and lightning in late afternoon. My father told stories of neighborhood men killed by lightning on tractors or horses, but he seemed to stay out in the storms longer than necessary for a man so sure of their power to kill.

As an adult, I wondered if his challenge to lightning was the only way he allowed himself to shake his fist at heaven, a fatalistic dare. Above all other lessons, ranchers learn patience with the unalterable: with blizzards during calving season, with lightning that kills one expensive bull in a pasture full of elderly cows, with rains that tear out fences. Ranch life is so crowded with chances for disaster that counting the awful possibilities could paralyze us if we allowed ourselves fear.

One of my father's mottoes was "What can happen, will." He never screamed curses when machinery broke down or calves brought less money in fall than we spent raising them. He faced whatever came, allowing himself only one terror, one chance to act out the anxiety he must have felt. A single wasp buzzing around his head on a summer day could move him out of his regular pace and make him dance. Ducking and weaving, he'd wave his handkerchief at the insect, hopping back and forth, his loose-jointed height almost graceful. He admitted his fear of wasps without embarrassment, my first lesson that even the brave are allowed fright.

But he declined to fear thunderstorms. At fifteen, I once refused to ride my horse after a cow because the black clouds were low and webbed with lightning, and I'd already heard a lot of stories about lightning striking the highest moving object, usually a horse and rider. My father's lips tightened, and we got in the pickup to find the cow. He ordered me to bring her in on foot and drove away as I ducked lightning flashes. When hail started a few minutes later, the cow tried to turn her back to it. I slapped her in the face, yelled, ducked in front of her. When I finally got the cow to the corral, both of us were covered with mud.

If my father was haying when a thunderstorm advanced, he kept wrestling the tractor with its creaking stacker around the field. On the mower, I'd forget to watch the falling alfalfa and fix my eyes on the bubbling underside of the dark clouds overhead. Each time his tractor neared the truck, I'd reach for my ignition key only to see the stacker teeth dropping again, scooping up another windrow of hay. As the machine lumbered back toward the stack, I'd shove the throttle ahead, driving faster on the next round, shoulders hunched, expecting a blast between my shoulder blades.

I always noticed that more birds swarmed around my head just before a storm. When my mower drove insects out of the protective vegetation into the winds before the storm, they dived into the falling alfalfa to snatch them. I felt like a whirlwind, beating up insects to be devoured.

My father would finally pull up beside the stack only after a lightning bolt had plummeted into the hill less than a mile from us. I'd lift the sickle bar, shift into fifth gear, and race toward him. Shouting to be heard over the thunder, we'd cover the tractors' exhaust stacks with tin cans and dash to the truck. Heading home through the field, he would drive around stands of uncut alfalfa, unwilling even in his hurry to damage a single stalk. Beside the truck in the garage, we'd stand panting a minute, hoping the rain might let up before we bolted for the house. By the time we stumbled inside, electricity would be bursting into fireworks over the barn roof and my mother would be huddled in the dark bedroom, shrieking every time the thunder rolled.

Once inside, Father would walk from window to window, watching lightning buffet the hillsides, afraid of a prairie fire. I'd follow him. In a year when ample winter snowfall and spring rain meant a heavy harvest, he'd tell yarns about storms he'd seen as a boy, how the horses ran away with one of his brothers and tipped the mower over. If the clouds dropped down gray and boiling with water, bringing a flood that scoured the earth instead of soaking into the dry soil, he'd say, "Well, anyway, it filled the big dam. Tore out the fence, though."

Watching a windy storm in a dry year, he'd set his mouth grimly and stare out the windows as a bolt struck. "That's a fire starter," he'd say. I'd strain my eyes watching for smoke. Either lightning would start a fire, or it wouldn't. If it did, either the rain would put it out or it wouldn't. If the rain didn't put it out, either the volunteer fire fighters would or they wouldn't. In several ways, we might lose the summer's hay already in the stack or the standing hay we hadn't yet cut. Neither anger nor fear would change the odds or the outcome.

Any summer storm could bring hail. During the hours my father paced the rooms with me trotting at his side, we'd listen rigidly for the first thump on the roof. A truly destructive hail always seemed to begin with one loud whack, followed by a long pause. We'd look at one another. One of us would guess at the size of that single hailstone. My father always raised his eyebrows and tilted his head as if the next stone's impact might be inaudible.

The second blow always shocked me. I'd jump as my mother screamed. Others followed quickly, like a drummer testing his skins before the concert, warming up for the *1812 Overture*. We'd stand silent at the big picture window as jagged chunks of ice battered leaves and branches from the trees, bounced on the driveway, chopped at the base of the tall yard grass we hadn't had time to mow. We never stated the obvious: that any crops not yet gathered were gone.

At such times, the prairie outside the window looked like an ocean with wet gusts rattling the windows and gray sheets of water sweeping across the landscape. We couldn't see more than a few feet beyond the glass. Occasionally, the murk would lift so we could glimpse one of the huge old cottonwoods east of the house, branches flailing against the wind.

Above the clothesline during that first storm, I glimpsed movement, the outline of a bird, wings beating furiously. I cried out, sure it would be battered to death by the hail.

"Oh, that's a nighthawk," my father said. A moment later I saw the distinctive white spots on its wings. Instead of flying into shelter or letting the wind take it south, the bird continued to flap in place. Watching, I thought of standing in a hot shower, how I raised both arms, bent my neck, turned in every direction so blessed heat could pound muscle aches. The thunderbird seemed to be doing the same, except that it required tremendous energy to remain stable against a fifty-mile-an-hour wind. For a quarter hour it raced and capered furiously in one position.

After that, I always saw the nighthawks cavorting in gales, noticed how they appeared before the rain to hunt above the wind-beaten grass.

As the nighthawks' flight became familiar, I was able to spot them anywhere on the plains with one sweeping glance at the broad sky. Down low, they fly like other birds, with even, rhythmic wing strokes against the air. But hunting nighthawks alter the tempo. Using several brisk strokes alternating with slower wing beats to lift their bodies, they mount the sky with a jerky motion, uttering a single high note, until they are barely visible. Then from high overhead the nighthawk drops silently. At the end of the dive it swoops up and a peculiar boom reverberates.

How, I wondered, do they make that eerie tone? Does it come from their throats or is it produced by the intricate wing motions demanded to curb that furious dive and soar again? One source says the wings produce "a peculiar musical hum" in the courtship dive, but I also heard the sound on summer nights as dozens of the birds, both adults and adolescents, hunted around my eaves. Several books I consulted fail to mention the sound at all, yet it's the surest way to identify the flying acrobat of the prairie, even in darkness. No other prairie creature makes a similar noise.

Birds of prey—true hawks—drop from the sky hard and fast to drive spiked talons into the spines of rabbits, the shock killing animals larger than themselves. Nighthawks dive to catch insects on the wing, so the practice is called hawking.

Riding after cattle, I sometimes saw a nighthawk's refuge—no one could sensibly call it a nest. The bird simply lays two eggs blotched with shades of green on an outcropping of limestone. The rough, lichen-covered stone camouflages the eggs and perhaps holds warmth while the parents hunt.

When George and I walked in our windbreak, a single nighthawk might flutter up from the ground just ahead, and we'd glimpse one mottled egg beside a downy chick, both yellow splotched with green. Invariably, the adult drifting just above the tallest grass tricked our eyes away. When we looked again, the chick was invisible, yet two more steps might crush it. Once we knew the locale of a nest, we avoided it for a month. One evening in late summer we'd notice nighthawks that seemed clumsy, then see a hovering adult and know another generation had survived.

During long twilights without George, I sat by the stone cairn on the hillside, watching the sun suck daylight past the western hills. Hidden in the tall grass, I became invisible—or insignificant—to nighthawks swooping after millers, mosquitoes, and grasshoppers. As darkness deepened, it seemed to breathe nighthawk sounds.

————

While Jerry visited with our friends, I stood at the back fence watching the nighthawks until the sky grew so dark I could see nothing, only hear an occasional boom as one dived. After Jerry grilled hamburgers, we attended a bluegrass concert, stomping to the music with an auditorium full of people. The fiddle strokes of

"Cotton-Eyed Joe" pulsed through the hall, music so perfect I closed my eyes. I could see the pure notes spiral and glide beneath the domed ceiling like nighthawks flying high and sweet. The music resonated in my bones, rang in each nerve and muscle. I shivered and looked at Jerry's watch: 10 P.M. At that moment, in the ranch kitchen three hundred miles away, my father collapsed and died.

His funeral followed one of the richest haying seasons in years. A crowd of ranchers gathered in the August heat, telling each other in undertones how many tons of hay they'd stacked and how much more they might cut if this warm weather lasted. The minister was a stranger to me, an immense woman in flowing robes. This splendid female looked like an ancient goddess carved in alabaster, but she chanted like an old-time evangelist at a tent revival.

Head bowed, I tried to look somber, but I expected my father to sit up in his coffin. "Christ!" he'd say. "What the hell is going on?" He detested fat and often declared that women belonged at home raising children. This minister incarnated almost everything he hated.

Swaying in her robes, the parson sang with the choir and led the assembled herd in prayers. Then she read from Genesis 2:8:

> And the Lord God planted a garden eastward in Eden; and there he put the man whom he had formed.

Above my father's casket, the minister's voice soared, resonating among the rafters, and she declared that the man God established in Eden was a rancher, but that the ranching business didn't really begin until God created woman to help him. "John's wife and daughter knew that," she intoned. "His daughter even wrote a book about her father and her love for the land and called it *Going Over East*. Her father refused to read it. He wouldn't even read his daughter's words about her love for this land. Remember, ladies and gentlemen, the hand of God moves in mysterious ways."

Stunned, I glanced at my mother. She shook her head, frowning. In the pew ahead of me, Margaret turned her head a little and winked. I stared at the casket, remembering when my father had read the preface of my first book, *Windbreak*. As soon as he saw that I'd referred to him as my "stepfather," he stopped reading, before he got to my explanation that he was the only father I'd ever known. He refused to read another word of my work. I'd tucked a complete set of my published books into the casket beside him that morning.

As the final prayers began, I put my arm around Mother. The fragile curve of her spine cut sharply into my arm. Old men with sunburned faces took off their hats. Among pallid foreheads and white skulls, we all recited:

The Lord is my Shepherd; I shall not want.

He maketh me to lie down in green pastures.

Beside the open grave on the cemetery hill, funeral home officials had set three wobbly folding chairs. By the time Jerry and I got there, a mortician had helped Mother out of the official limousine and seated her. Sunlight made her skin transparent, her veins flushing purple. Margaret stood nearby, her face weary. Hugging her, I led her to the chair beside me. "He's gone to open the gates for the rest of us," she whispered.

The preacher's royal robes lifted and surged in the prairie wind as she paced up the hill. The solemn phrases of the prayer rolled up and dissipated. Head raised, I admired the supple gold curves of hay stacks in our fields along the creek.

Six of my cousins lowered my father's casket. One helped my mother into his car and left for the post-funeral feeding ritual at the community hall. Jerry visited with several old ranchers who leaned against their pickups while their wives stared out through the windshields.

As I walked with Margaret to her car, she told me about a dream she'd had the night before. "We were driving somewhere together. Not to some boring environmental meeting. Somewhere we were happy to be going. I was looking out the window and hollered at you to pull off the road. We got out of the car and looked up. Above us were nineteen flocks of white birds circling. I counted very carefully, exactly nineteen flocks of birds, all white." She smiled up at me, her pale face radiant. "What do you think that means?" She chuckled. "Think you should start going to church?"

Margaret and her family drove away, and Jerry took my mother to the church. I turned back to the graves where my friend Tom, source of my information about the HIV virus, stood at the foot of the fresh mound of earth. I took his arm and leaned against his shoulder. He said, "There's just one space between your father and George."

"The tradition here is to bury the husband on the north," I explained. "So I'll be south of George and then my mother south of my dad."

"You'll be between George and your father?" He looked at me, eyebrows high. "Between them?"

We goggled at each other. "Yes! Right where I didn't want to be when they were alive!"

He gulped. "I hope they get along better then. Too bad you'll be dead and won't know."

"The *good* news is that I'll be dead," I gasped, and we both gave up the effort to contain our laughter and clung to each other, gurgling and snorting, while the leftover mourners stared.

Looking for Life: Fire in the Wildlife Pasture

A few years ago, one of our neighbors hired an old man to build a new set of corrals beside the highway. The whole community found a reason to pass the site daily, appraising the work as the stringy old cowboy set posts and nailed up planks. Most of us knew the back-wrenching strain of having to lift a wooden gate that has sagged with age, so we noticed how he braced the heavy gates so they'd swing smoothly. Later, several neighbors asked him to do fencing for them and he found steady work for a dozen nearby ranches. The new pine planks of the finished corrals shone like gold bars against tar-black posts. The rancher grouped twenty-five stacks of hay—his whole summer's harvest—next to the fence, ready for winter feeding.

My father shook his head as we drove by one day. "Shouldn't crowd those stacks," he said. "One cigarette out of a car window, one lightning strike, could take 'em all. That's why I scatter my stack yards and take the chance it will be harder to get to some of them if the snow's deep."

Lightning struck one of the stacks during an August hailstorm. By the time neighbors and volunteer fire fighters arrived, stacks and corrals were burning. Another pitch plank or post exploded every few seconds. We could do nothing but circle the fire, watching, wetting the surrounding grass.

We all saw the old man arrive, knew he owned neither the hay nor the corrals. Cursing, he filled buckets from a water truck and ran through the inferno, throwing water. Each time he disappeared in black smoke, he was gone longer before he emerged, coughing. Several times he appeared and fell to his knees. As soon as he could stand, he filled his bucket and ran back.

We sympathized so deeply with his desire to save the corrals and with his right to act—even foolishly, even without hope—we almost waited too long. Finally, two men caught his arms and dragged him away.

He rebuilt the corrals before the first snowfall. Whenever neighbors discussed the incident, they nodded approval as they ended the story. He was one of us, adhering to tradition: to rebuild, to recover, no matter how terrible the disaster. Maybe I don't belong on the ranch anymore.

Freedom begins between the ears.

—Edward Abbey
A Voice Crying in the Wilderness

As the fella said, 'Cheer up, it could be worse.'
So I cheered up, and sure enough, it got worse.

—Saying frequently repeated by
John Hasselstrom during 1992

Here in Cheyenne I look out the window and notice thick frost coating the windshield of my car. It is early December, and dried wildflowers prattle in a chill wind. Shivering, I pace between the dining room and living room, drinking coffee and watching cars pass. I'm in no hurry to head upstairs, where my desk is piled high with my father's papers, but I can't sit still.

My accountant has located more than fifty separate accounts in my father's name, making it my job to trace when he bought each investment and how much he paid so we can consolidate them for my mother. In many cases, she isn't listed as a joint owner, further complicating the job. Some of the ranch land, most of the machinery, the cattle, even his brand, carry only my father's name. Beside envelopes full of receipts is a stack of papers outlining my lawyer's suggestion that we set up a trust fund to support my mother. Determining just what she has inherited, and how it can best serve her needs, will be my full-time job for the next four years.

My father's will mentioned me only to note he was leaving me nothing. Though Mother has never even reconciled her own checkbook, she was named executor. I try to tell myself that my father knew she would relinquish the job to me. I want to believe this was his way of admitting he was wrong, making me responsible for my mother and the ranch. I'm lying to myself. Either he really believed she was capable of sorting out the mess he left, or he was sure she'd find a man to do it for her.

I seat myself before the pile, but in a few moments, I'm pacing the hallway again, looking out upstairs windows. My hands are clenched. When I get back to my study, I stand looking down at my car, fighting the urge to jump into it and head for the ranch. Jerry called from his office to tell me roads to the north are drifted and icy. I have no reason to go. So what causes my anxiety?

My father has been dead five months, but I'm too busy and too angry to mourn. Besides documenting his investments, we've got to prepare income tax statements. His last journal, full of names and physical descriptions of neighbors he'd known for forty years, is stuffed with receipts to sort. Much as he hated my writing, he wrote to brace himself as the foundations of his world shifted. Words were his only shield against events he could not control or judge.

My mother insisted on going to Texas, to the apartment my parents had rented in previous winters. When I refused to drive her, she bought a plane ticket. At the airport, I helped her hobble to the loading gate. As a stewardess pushed her out the door in a wheelchair, she called, "Take care of my cats and my plants."

She wouldn't let me find a winter caretaker for her house. When I lived at the ranch, I could check the furnace daily, build a fire in the wood stove, leave faucets running. Even then, the water in the toilet bowl froze solid one night a few years ago when the thermometer hit forty below zero and the electricity was off. I told her that I might not be able to get to the ranch, but she waved me away. The couple renting my house will check hers periodically. Since the woman works in town and the man stays at home, writing, perhaps they will spot trouble before it becomes serious. Maybe mother is living in the blithe assumption that someone will take care of her because someone always has.

Mother wrote me every day in previous winters, but as she loses track of herself, her scribbled notes are repetitive and rare. She calls every Sunday at the same time to tell me the same things: she went to church, she went shopping, her next-door neighbor walked with her to the café, where she ate the same steak. When I call the neighbor, she assures me Mother is doing fine. That can't be entirely true, but I'm relieved to know she's in Texas instead of living alone at the ranch.

What else could be wrong? The fire danger is higher than usual for this late in the season and the pastures around the ranch are still covered with tall brown grass. As Margaret always says, "We're surrounded by acres and acres of fuel." From her kitchen window, my aunt Jo used to see most of our big prairie fires start when train engines blew sparks into the long grass. After Josephine died, Margaret nominated me unofficial fire lookout because Windbreak House stands high enough on the hill to overlook the railroad tracks. "You don't need to keep track of the gossip, though," she added, giggling as we recalled Jo's reputation of knowing everything about everyone, and telling most of it to anyone who would listen.

Working in my basement study in fire season, I always worried about not being able to see the northern horizon. If a fire started in the most likely spot beside the railroad tracks, I might not see it before it engulfed the house. I usually took a break every hour to walk outside, looking around and sniffing the wind. Will Al, who now uses my basement study, think to do the same? The last time I visited the ranch, the renters, Al and Jill, invited me into my house, and I had to clasp my hands together and lock my jaws to speak calmly. No, I said, they could not paint the living room walls black.

Margaret is now bedridden with the effects of the HIV virus, and a nurse comes in daily to help care for her. I'd call her, but it's too early for the nurse to be there, and Margaret may be too weak to answer the phone. She could hardly hold it during our last conversation. Her voice was a whisper.

Settling at the desk again, I shuffle papers until the phone rings. I race into the bedroom, snatching it after the first ring. "Do you want the good news or the bad news first?"

Biting back my usual response to anyone who starts talking without offering an identity, I recognize the voice of Jill, the renter. "The good news," I say. "Haven't had much lately."

"Al got out of the house. He said the grass was on fire in every direction he looked."

Fire. Prairie fire.

"Is my house gone? My folks' house?"

"I don't know," she says. "He called me from Hermosa. Said he'd been writing and when he looked outside, the fire was so close he threw the cat and his manuscript in the car and ran. In Hermosa, he called the fire department and the guy who rents the land."

While she babbles, I stand with the phone to my ear, picturing his panicky flight. Seeing flames encircle my horizon, I tally fire-fighting equipment as if I were in my own house, automatically mapping the shortest route to each tool. I imagine jumping in my car, racing to the ranch. I'd load old cream cans full of cloth feed bags, put them in the pickup and fill each can with water. At the fire, I'd swing a waterlogged bag at the base of the flames, beating out sparks and flames a few feet at a time. Hour after hour I'd work, replacing dry or shredded sacks until the fire was out. Adrenaline pumps through me and my shoulders ache as I remember the weight of a wet sack at the end of my arm.

Smoke has always been our signal to race toward a prairie fire, no matter whose land was threatened. I hope my neighbors are helping the volunteer fire fighters save those two houses around which most of my memories center. I hope it isn't too late.

What can I do? If I were at the ranch, I'd dash into my house and start grabbing things. But even in good weather, the drive from Cheyenne to the ranch takes five hours. By the time I got there, the fire might be out. The neighbors will stop it as they've done before. If it can be stopped.

All his life, my father squeezed every drop of value from each penny. If the house he built for us has burned, all my parents' possessions are gone. These confused records of their scrimping might be all that survives.

Replacing the telephone receiver, I hear a hymn playing on the radio: "Hark the Herald Angels Sing." When I stood in the congregation in the little white church in Hermosa on Christmas Eve, I was always puzzled by the words "sad and lowly plains." To me, those plains are heaven.

In warm boots and a heavy coat, I take Frodo to the park, where a lively wind blows hamburger wrappings and snow around our legs. I stare up at bare trees, head spinning, seeing the shelves in the basement of my house as clearly as if a burning wall has fallen away. My unfinished novels, George's rifle. I hear the fire snap. My eyes sting as if the house's ashes are floating out of the city sky.

Frodo and I are both shivering when I drive to the grocery store and post office. Standing in slow-moving lines, I wonder what would happen if I screamed at blank-faced strangers, "Everyone I love is dead and my house is burning down!"

By the time I return to the house in late afternoon, the prosaic shopping chore has calmed me, in spite of remembering a conversation I had had with the writer living in my ranch house. I warned him that the railroad trains often start fires north of my house, explaining how he should water the windbreak trees on that side of the house to provide a fire break. After several talks, he looked puzzled and said, "You're always telling me where things are by direction, but I don't know which way is which. And what's a fire break?" I wonder whether the fire was north or south of my house. No use asking the renters.

On a late-fall visit to the ranch, I asked Al to roll up a hose lying under the front porch. The next time I was there, I noticed carpet I'd used to mulch the trees scattered between the rows. He'd ripped three hundred feet of plastic water pipe out of the windbreak. Said it was a helluva job. The garden hose still lay under the porch.

If the fire is south of the ranch houses, I am probably worrying over nothing because the wind usually comes from the north. Margaret has a police radio in her kitchen so she will know, even though she's busy dying. I dial her number to hear her voice, familiar but thinner than last week. The fire started north of me but she's positive my place is safe. She's not sure about my folks' house.

For several hours, I sit with Frodo on my lap, staring at the photograph of my Bronco in the tall grass, recalling my parents' house.

Inside the oak buffet in the dining room stands the china dinner service, the welcoming gift that the Ladies Aid gave to my mother when she married John. Yellowed tablecloths and potholders are stacked on the shelves below the plates—pieces my grandmother crocheted in the lonely winters of her second widowhood. In the buffet's bottom drawer lie Grandmother's frail tablecloths and doilies, like thin ancestral bones in a charnel house.

On the other side of the bathroom doorway, a closet holds three worn-out irons and four toasters, along with a book on electrical repair—right where my father could grab them after he found the time to learn about electrical repairs. In a far back corner lies an old black-and-white home movie. Jerky scenes show my mother on the beach in Galveston, Texas, holding me as a two year old. When the camera focused on my birthday party that year, a small, dark-haired boy tried to take my paper hat. I socked him in the nose and smirked while he bawled. My biological father, Paul, appeared among the tussling children laughing and holding high a glass of whiskey.

Itemizing what might be lost in my parents' house, I see deep shelves holding boxes of clothes I outgrew in high school and a box of mending that's grown larger every year. On top are three new shirts in Christmas wrap my father will never wear. The day I first saw Mother sewing a tuck in the left sleeve of each of his shirts, she told me he'd had rheumatic fever as a child, leaving him with one arm shorter and weaker than the other. I asked him about it only once. "I hated being a cripple," he said, glowering. I nearly laughed—I'd never even noticed the small difference, hardly crippling. Still, that small defect, coupled with his slight frame and thick glasses, may have made him an outcast in our rural community, subject to teasing by big, healthy boys like Harold. Perhaps damage invisible to me was an eternal grievance.

Next to the mending box are twine-wrapped bundles of paper scraps my father used to figure his taxes for the past few years, along with envelopes stuffed with pedigrees from long-dead bulls and investment statements. Some of the recent information is now piled around my desk. Envelopes full of paid bills, check stubs, and old income tax returns filled three tight metal garbage cans in the storm cellar. I brought to Cheyenne the bundle of small black notebooks held together with a rubber band, his diaries since the 1950s. I have them in a box in the basement, along with those my mother has kept since she was nine years old. So far, I'm too angry to read them.

Those overcrowded shelves epitomize my parents' lives: collections of objects that might be usable, hoarded because waste is a sin. People who lived through the hungry years of the thirties might understand why my father kept a tin box filled with old spark plugs and cracked fuses. Behind the box, I found the fringed cowboy shirt Mother bought me for my ninth birthday, tucked into a bread wrapper. Besides souvenirs I can understand, and every penny they made, my parents hoarded anything, no matter how fragmented, that represents their history—like the cracked cut-glass pitcher in the buffet. It was special to someone, but no one ever told me its significance and my mother doesn't remember.

On the living room shelves stand my favorite childhood books, none so worn as *Ferdinand the Bull* and *The White Stag*. On the same shelves are the Faulkner novels I brought home after a college seminar, bristling with scraps of newspaper, my father's usual bookmark. He never stopped surprising me with what he recalled.

Between the books are shoeboxes bulging with hundreds of envelopes filled with photographs my mother has vowed to put in albums every winter of my memory. In one picture I recognize the dim face of my grandmother standing on a city sidewalk, prim in her long, black wool coat. I look closely at the child holding her hand and know those skinned knees at once. I loved speeding on my roller skates and never properly learned to stop. In the guest room, I found a huge steamer trunk filled with more ancient photographs.

I considered moving all these remnants of my parents' lives to the basement of my own house, but I didn't trust my tenants. I might have moved them to Cheyenne, but my trips back and forth have been so hectic I kept putting the job off. Perhaps I was not quite ready to admit that I live in Cheyenne so completely that I've brought my annals with me. Our whole family history may burn. All my life I've felt responsible not only for each day's labor but for keeping track of the stories representing my past. I sense a tingle of relief: perhaps the obligation will vanish with no blame to me. Family pictures might turn to ash, fragile shadows as insubstantial as the solid bodies they represent.

Late in the night, after calling a half dozen friends and relatives, I confirm that the fire has missed our buildings. High winds are catapulting flames east and south toward the Cheyenne River. Winter grass and haystacks are gone, cattle have been singed and smothered. But no one has died. No one has lost a home. Harold, nearly ninety and living alone since Aunt Josephine died, has endured in his life all that bucking horses and South Dakota weather could do to him. He says wearily, "It burned the heart out of my winter pasture."

Al tells me he was working in my basement study and thought he heard me shout, "Danger! Danger!" Running outside, he saw the horizon ablaze. Later, he learned that high winds blew down a power pole, breaking a wire and causing sparks that set the flames. He reasons that the break caused an electric surge that triggered my answering machine.

My recorded message said nothing about danger. The mundane explanation doesn't convince either of us. Before trouble threatened that land where I grew up, three hundred miles away, I was already twitching with alarm.

I doze in a chair, dreaming of riding horseback on a neighbor's land I always call the wildlife pasture. In winter it shelters a band of deer with a circular territory two or three miles in diameter. For years, I've watched old does in the same band of deer teach younger ones the secrets of moving down the draw below my house to water there. They tiptoe among the willows growing at the bottom of the gully until they can cross the railroad tracks to the east, learning the land wrinkle by wrinkle, as I did. In the trees of another sheltered ravine, I've lain on my back watching great horned owls and golden eagles. From a limestone shelf I've studied ripples as turtles dug into the muddy bottoms of pools. Porcupines scrambled under the cliffs when I rode by. Neighbors drove cattle to safety ahead of the flames, but what about the owl, the deer, the turtles?

Miles of slick roads and shifting drifts prevent me from getting home, even to mourn. Deep in the night, while I nap in a pool of electric light—carried by wires like the one that started the fire— snow falls on the burned land. I can see it behind my eyelids as clearly as if I am there. One by one, white flakes fall until the black ashes are veiled.

Badger's Daughter

No matter how many decisions I made about the ranch, I always drove north from Cheyenne to visualize the impact of every last one of them. Gut twisting, I debated every alternative along the way, conducting a running argument with my father for the whole five-hour trip. Each time I drove down the lane from the highway, his faded red cap would catch my eye as he stepped into the dark barn or bent to water the oak tree in the yard. I tallied each loose wire, each missing shingle on the barn roof. When I saw a wire gate lying on the ground, I stopped to prop it against the fence so it wouldn't be buried in snow or growing grass. "See how well I'm doing?" I'd ask my father. Sometimes I almost convinced myself that I heard him do the unthinkable—apologize for his anger. I never quite believed I heard him say he loved me.

In late fall, nighthawks often settle on dirt or asphalt roads to warm themselves with the day's hoarded heat. Driving north, I always saw them smashed on the highway, upright wings fluttering like mourning banners, little flags whispering greetings from wind that had carried them high.

One evening, as I topped the hill on the entrance road to the ranch, a nighthawk rose before the car. I braked and dimmed my headlights. The nighthawk flew ahead of me as the car crept slowly forward.

The nighthawk's wings rose and fell, lifted and dropped. With each beat, the white patch in the center of each wing swept in a half arc, so

every stroke sketched a shining circle. The shimmering wings created a
hoop of light around the bird's dark body. In darkness, the nighthawk
flew onward inside a glimmering halo of pure grace.

> Bear Claw:
> You've come far, pilgrim.
>
> Jeremiah Johnson:
> Feels like far.
>
> Bear Claw:
> Were it worth the trouble?
>
> Jeremiah Johnson:
> Ahh—what trouble?
>
> —JEREMIAH JOHNSON

I'll be glad to see the year end. This gray December morning I sat
in my Cheyenne dining room longer than usual with my coffee, trying to prepare my mind for what the prairie fire did to my familiar
landscape before I headed north to see. After fighting similar fires
for forty years, I could picture the buffalo grass charring into gray
ash, curling into the ground as if to protect its roots. If the fire
moved fast enough to destroy old growth and weed seeds, leaving
the roots of the native grasses unharmed, the pastures may benefit.
The weather in Wyoming looked threatening, but Jerry checked
with his highway buddies and warned me about icy and snow-

packed stretches before I sped north under low-hanging clouds. This is likely my last trip this winter.

I stop my car in my parents' driveway, and I walk through the silent ranch yard. Did the curtain move at the dining room window? I study the shaky sheds and overgrown weeds as if they are new to me. I assemble a mental list of repairs that must be done, as if everything here is my responsibility.

I am buying the ranch from my mother. My name will soon be on the deeds, but have I lost the title to my prairie life? It's too late for me to raise children here, and I may never live here again. My family's life, woven into this land for a hundred years, is gone. In September, not long after my father died, I copied into my journal these lines from David Quammen's "Natural Acts" column in *Outside* magazine:

> A whirlpool is one type of vortex. Hurricanes and little prairie-wind twisters. . . . The full-curl horns on a bighorn ram represent vortical growth, as does the shell of a chambered nautilus.

Sauntering in the sunshine, I feel I'm floating on the outside edge of the whirlpool, where the water slows. Death washed away the solid bedrock of my life as I drove back and forth across the plains this year. My father and George, who tied me to this place, are subsiding into the land. Even asleep, I can feel my body spinning. Are these changes in my life vortical growth? Or the destructive confusion of a prairie twister?

Like a wily cow ducking through a gate ahead of the rancher on horseback, my brain seizes this chance to shuffle through different meanings for the word *twist*. My father used the word to mean the joint between a cow's thigh and her lower leg. When he said, "She's down in the twist," he meant the cow was so badly injured she seldom got up again. "I may be down in the twist myself," I say to the dead elm tree by the big corral. When I open the little gate by the barn, it pitches sideways, dangling from a broken hinge and reminding me that the flat part of a hinge is also called a twist. We call fierce prairie winds twisters even if a weather prophet terms them tornadoes. My grandmother manipulated her crochet needles while she taught me that "twist" referred to a cord spun or braided from several threads. English poets of the 1600s wrote of "spinning the twist of life" as they reflected on death.

Leaning against the barn, faded to the same faint pink as my father's cap, I recall my meeting with the men who control my life for the foreseeable future: my lawyer, an accountant, a bank officer, and a real estate agent.

First the bank officer explained how we might construct a trust to serve my mother's needs while absolving me of financial responsibility for her.

Then the real estate broker, who'd appraised the ranch for probate, announced briskly that he'd found a buyer for the cattle and the ranch—a good offer considering the serious disrepair of the buildings and fences.

I looked around the table. All four men wore looks of benign pleasure and expectancy. I asked, "What are my other options?" They looked at each other. "Have any of you gentlemen read my books?" I asked gently, knowing the answer. Of course not. Their professions and their private lives are separate. They'd never realized that a rancher's work encircles her home, as does the labor of a writer.

My lawyer looked chagrined. He's been my friend since college days and handled my divorce from my first husband, so every time I've published a book, I've sent him a signed copy.

As the men shifted in their chairs and cleared their throats, I recited to myself a motto attributed to Mother Jones, "Pray for the dead and fight like hell for the living," saying aloud, "Unless it is the only way to provide for my mother, selling the land is not an option."

During the discussion that followed, we found a way for me to buy the ranch and simultaneously save my mother enormous inheritance taxes. To pay my father's debts and set up the trust, I sold most of my father's cow herd and the new truck he found so confusing. To pay the expenses of probate and the land taxes, I sold my own cattle and borrowed money from my mother. That won't be enough to repair fences and corrals my father has been cobbling together with baling wire for ten years. No one can guess what those expenses might be or whether this scheme will work.

I've leased the land to my neighbor, the man who has worked for my uncle Harold for fifteen years and is buying his ranch. Cattle prices have dropped in recent years, so he may not be able to earn or borrow enough money to buy my uncle's ranch while leasing mine. We may both scrimp and plot for another ten years and still lose both ranches.

I have been practicing saying "my ranch." I repeat it aloud, scuffing dry cow chips in the corral. The place feels deserted, as if it's been empty for years. Most of the cows wearing my father's brand and mine are still here, grazing the deep grass over east—but they now belong to my neighbor. When I see them in our pastures, I know them by their history with me. If I told their new owner about The Cow That Bashed Her Baby Around the Limestone Outcrop, for example, the story would have no meaning to him. He may know her as The Cow That Kicked Him in the Head While He Tried to Milk Her. Since he doesn't know our stories about her ancestry, he may call Ugly's great granddaughter simply The Cow That Raises the Biggest Calf Every Year. He is composing his own legends around the cattle and this land. I've heard him repeat the stories he heard from my uncle Harold, tales that originated fifty years before either of us lived here.

To save confusion when he sells cows or calves wearing our brands, my neighbor bought both my father's Bar 99 brand, registered to commemorate the year his father proved up his homestead, and my Heartbreak Hotel brand. Gradually, as those cows age, he'll replace them with younger cows wearing his own brands. He has promised to sell both brands back to me when our cows are finally gone. I've watched wealthy urbanites buy old branding irons at auctions to decorate their homes in western style. Will I someday hang my family's branding irons on a wall, as if they are only decorations?

I have several children—technically stepchildren from my two marriages—but none is interested in the ranch or ranching. I have no one to whom I can pass along all I know about ranching on this land. Some wisdom requires a taste of soil, the scent of a blizzard in a particular wind. If I moved back to the ranch, found an apprentice, and worked here with her for the rest of my life, much of what I know might endure. But that will not happen.

Whoever occupies this land after I die will understand little of its history. She won't know where to take shelter, walking home in chilly rain when the pickup's stuck in that nasty mud hole in the summer pasture. He won't understand that the willow patch below my house really belongs to the old doe and her daughters. In thirty or forty years, a new owner might learn some basics—might even manage to build a herd as well adapted to this place as ours—if his ownership lasted that long. As real estate prices and property taxes climb, land is still considered a good investment, so the turnover can be quick.

Harold wanted to give his ranch to the man who is leasing mine, and who worked for him for so long, but federal income tax laws won't allow that. Community gossips were shocked that he was not leaving it to relatives, "keeping it in the family." His answer was a growl, "I didn't spend seventy years on this place so it could be somebody's damn investment. I want a family to live here, the way mine did."

Living with integrity on this land will require more than a new name on the deeds. Land is the basis of community. Successful stewardship means learning all one can from previous inhabitants, including the animals. By the time I learned the lineage of all our cows, they were more than walking legal tender—all they represented to my mother. In winter, when I lived alone here, I walked among those cows, patting shoulders and flanks, talking softly and rubbing ears. When roads drifted closed and telephone lines dropped, the cows became my family, recognizing me as surely as I knew them. Our relationship was more like a civilized exchange than an ownership of one by the other. Working with the cows in pastures filled with native animals helped me assimilate ways of living responsibly and with enjoyment in the country. When I ran to head one off at a gate, I judged her intention with the same measure I use to determine what a person will do: by her expression, by the look in her eye. I can't determine the future of the ranch the same way.

When my father criticized or belittled me, he defended his abuse as part of teaching me to toughen up. If anyone else badmouthed me, he spoke up. "We can bicker inside the family," he'd say, "but we stick together." At family gatherings, he'd listen with a half smile as relatives recited their children's accomplishments. Then, head cocked to one side, one eyebrow raised, he always said, "Linda's not much, but she's all we've got."

I face the sagging barn and inhale. "Just remember," I bellow, "I'm all you've got."

———

In mid-December, two weeks after the prairie fire, I dream of a gate. Not the native ironwood gate sticks and barbed wire we use in the pastures but a noble gate framed in vertical bars of glowing light. Even submerged in my dream, I hesitate to stride between those radiant shafts. I look at my hands to see if they are clean enough to open it, realizing I am not ready to leave this world. Then I see two men inside: George and my father, both smiling. I falter, beginning to be angry. How can they look so serene while I am still snarled in the disorder of keeping the ranch solvent?

Sensing someone at my shoulder, I step politely aside. Margaret walks firmly past me. My husband and father offer their hands to her. Of course—Margaret is only forty-two, her closest relatives are all still living. Perhaps my father, who knew Margaret as a baby, and my husband, who knew how much I loved her, will be her companions and guides there, forgetting their hostility to each other.

I try to peek between the shining bars, wondering if it is truly paradise in the sense I define it: Is the grass high and green this year? The gates swing shut behind Margaret.

The phone wakes me at dawn. I raise the receiver to my ear, still hazy with the dream. Bill says, "Margaret's gone."

After George's death, Margaret wrapped her strong arms around me every time we met, but she died in pain so intense she couldn't bear to be touched. She asked that her body be cremated, the ashes scattered in her windbreak, but her father's wishes prevailed. The urn containing her ashes was buried where he wanted it, in a city cemetery where sprinklers run all day, sucking water from our fragile aquifers to keep the grass unnaturally green.

The day Margaret died, I took from my pantry a gallon jar of honey she gave me during her forty-second and final summer. Sugar crystals stood in hazy towers, as if she'd captured and gilded one of the cumulonimbus clouds we used to watch from my dining room window on fall days.

I filled a heavy kettle with warm water, placed the jar inside, and set the pan over a low flame. The water began to steam as a finger-width of liquid gold from dissolving crystals appeared at the bottom of the jar. With the long-handled wooden spoon—George carved it from a piece of alder he harvested at his grandfather's house in Michigan—I stirred the last fist-sized crystal into the warm honey. I placed the jar on the table beside a pot of tea, a dish of butter, and a pan of scones.

At the dining room table I sipped my tea alone, watching the dry stems of prairie coneflowers in the flowerbeds beside the street as they shivered in the wind. The bubbles in the honey floated slowly upward as I recalled our autumn conversations over tea and honey. Margaret once described how a hive swarms when the queen and her family leave to find new quarters. A new hive, like a human infant, requires constant attention and care to survive. Each hive progresses from adolescence to adulthood as it helps its queen grow up. Providing its own workers, the colony grows until it gives birth to new hives and ultimately, like a human, grows old and dies. Modern scholars believe a beehive is not simply a colony but a single animal "of many glittering parts." Just as a human family is bonded by blood, bees may be linked by honey flowing through each individual bee. United by sweetness, a hive of bees may be a single creature in action and in spirit. The way a family should be, the way a community might be.

In my study that morning, I had tried to write about Margaret, abandoning the effort to weep. That afternoon, I took old Frodo to my favorite Cheyenne park and ambled behind him around the lake, joining a parade of other middle-aged women with their elderly dogs. Overhead, I heard Margaret's laugh bubble through a skein of southbound geese. Ducks, like those she raised and freed, gabbled in the shallows of the pond. Walking under the eighty-foot trees thriving on city water, I imagined Margaret beside me, admiring the trees' height, speculating on whether her trees would ever grow so tall. I could hear her asking tough questions about the source and quantity of Cheyenne's water supply.

At other times, in the same park, I have heard George's cough from a stranger and missed him as sharply as if he had died yesterday. In Jackson Hole, I saw a track in the mud identical to the print of George's big foot. In the only flow of time that really matters, he had stepped into the sparkling willows just ahead of me. No wonder Frodo wanted to follow.

———

Lately I've glimpsed my father's lean figure pacing the banks of the lake, unable to relax. When I notice a straight-backed old man with a fishing pole, walking toward the lake with a loose-limbed, prairie-eating lope, I smile and say, "Good afternoon," remembering the childhood summer when my mother gave my father and me fishing poles for our birthdays. One day she packed us a picnic lunch and sent us to a creek in the Black Hills. My father sat for only a moment or two before he propped his pole up with a couple of rocks. While I sat on the bank, he stood behind me, hands in his pockets as he jingled his car keys and knife. Sometimes he walked back and forth, frowning and looking at his watch. I don't remember catching any fish. When we got home, he put our poles up on the rafters in the garage, where I found them not long ago. Perhaps in the country beyond the shining gate George and my father are friends, and George is teaching Father to fly fish, instructing him in the art of patience.

Epilogue: Spinning with the Hawks

Twice, far out in a pasture, I have seen a dark column rise from the pale buffalo grass. Water and DNA flow in spirals, as do sound and light, and tornadoes, all unlikely on this arid grassland. Perhaps I was seeing a bolt of pure energy ascending from earth to sky. Or the opposite: galaxies auguring star power into the ground. Magic. Angels coming to rescue or revenge.

Closer to the swirling shape, I was still puzzled. Maybe I was seeing a dust devil, though I doubted even a plains wind could suck dust from the thick grass where no one had ever plowed. Finally, my eyes focused on hundreds of birds flying in circles. Together, they formed a whirling shaft mounting the air: a hawk spiral. Bird watchers who only visit the prairie tell me such sightings are rare. I have seen hawk spirals twice.

I lay down on a little knoll, counting birds until I grew dizzy. The earth was warm as flesh beneath me. Long grass blew over me like ocean swells. Hundreds of wings whipped the air. Closing my eyes, I visualized torrents of air flowing outward from this center, covering the earth. The breath pouring into my lungs was power charged.

As hawks whirled slowly overhead, I memorized markings and shapes. Red-tailed hawks revolved around ferruginous and rough-legged hawks; merlins and kestrels skittered between. A peregrine falcon sailed the edges.

I picked one redtail to watch through a monocular as he flew straight into the base of the whirlwind. First he circled low, as if hunting, but each revolution took him higher. In a dozen rounds, he was halfway up the column of birds. Ten minutes later, he blasted out the top of the hoop and glided west, hunting. He drifted back and forth over a ridge until he paused, wings fluttering, and dropped on something in the grass.

Experts say the hawks are playing, showing off their skills for a specialized audience of other winged predators. Hawks spiral only when they migrate, traveling from one homeland—one part of their vast personal terrain—to another.

Stories spiraling like hawks at play define the history of any landscape, any people. The universe loops around and around, repeating itself. Perhaps we must watch or live the same story over and over again until we understand; perhaps we orbit until we learn diligence, until we choose to live our lives responsibly.

I think nobody owns land until their dead are in it.

—JOAN DIDION
River Run

Sometimes I dream that my grandmother Cora is braiding my hair, as she did when I lived with my mother in the little house in Rapid City. When I wake, I can still feel her strong, warm hands on my head. After my grandmother moved back to her ranch, my mother braided my hair for a week or two, yanking harder every day and mumbling under her breath. One Saturday she took me to a beauty parlor where a gum-chewing teenager hacked off the braids while I sobbed.

For years, condemned to wear my hair short because it was easier for Mother, I mourned my loss, telling friends how my golden hair once hung nearly to my waist. With gestures and sound effects, I recreated the heavy thump as each braid hit the floor. I could still hear it twenty years later.

My mother broke a bone in her back a year after my father died, and I moved her into a nursing home. Emptying her house for tenants, I spent days sorting through the stuff she'd saved, berating her in my mind for never throwing anything away. Far back in her cluttered dresser drawer, I found my braids, wrapped in a plastic bag. They were six inches long. Holding the two small hanks of hair, I stood in front of my mother's big mirror for a long time, blushing to think of all the times I'd told a lie.

All those years, I believed I was telling the truth. I was not conscious of deception. Did the hard evidence prove me wrong? Even with the little coils of hair in my hand, I could hear them hit the floor, the sound reverberating in my story. Short as those plaits were, they were most of the hair I had.

When I go to the little hilltop cemetery in Hermosa after a rain, I often spend a half hour sitting on George's tombstone, enjoying the view while I scrape yellow gumbo off my shoes, cursing its tenacity. Pioneers told how this primeval mud clogged wagon wheels so thickly that it pulled powerful teams of four oxen to a stop. Modern engineers can cover it with pavement, but if this soil absorbs enough water, the highways slide, and there is nothing technology can do to stop the disintegration.

Death and gumbo converge in my mind because all my dead are buried in the stuff. Flesh of our flesh mutates into sparse grass in these gumbo graveyards, with little help from heavenly water and none from underground. We are so careful to label each slice of earth, as if the name of the body buried there is significant. *Mitakuye oyasin,* say the Lakota, who were here before us: "All my relatives."

Every spring of my childhood my parents brought me to this spot to pull weeds from the graves of my father's ancestors. Afterward, Mother turned the hose on me in the yard, vainly trying to wash away the greasy stuff, while Father vacuumed the car. The next Sunday, we tended my mother's family graves in the southern Black Hills, coming back sticky with gumbo again.

Wandering among the dead, I recall the day we lowered Cora, my mother's mother, into her gumbo bed. She was the only one of my grandmothers I knew well. Since she died, I have heard her voice in my Cheyenne kitchen, reverberating among her bowls and wooden spoons, reminding me how to stuff turkeys and how much flour to add to the gravy. Yet the last time I visited the Edgemont cemetery, an hour south of where George lies, I couldn't find her grave. Every day, I use some tool her hands wore smooth, resurrecting her in kitchens she never saw, but I could not locate the narrow rectangle of earth that bears her name.

Hard rains and dry years have doubtless settled the earth over her brittle bones, cracking her casket open to let silt sift into the silk lining. "Blast that gumbo!" she'd say on wash day. "Once it gets on clothes, the stain never comes out." Now she lies mute under its weight, mouth sealed with clay.

In the years since George died, I have spent considerable time kneeling on his grave, planting flowers and pulling weeds. If Frodo came with me, I could always find him in the shade of a tough little juniper, one of the few trees in the graveyard. Now the cemetery association has outlawed planting trees because they heave coffins out of the ground and require more water than we can spare for the dead. By the time George died, we'd nurtured the trees and bushes around Windbreak House for nearly ten years, and in one way or another, I'd been planting and harvesting on the prairie—gardens, wildflowers, grass inside healthy calves, and books—for thirty years.

I'd honored the pledges we made to one another in marriage, and realized that in finishing that pact, I'd begun another: tending the leathery perennials above George's perishable flesh. On each visit, I scatter tobacco to the wind's four directions as the Lakota do, as George always did. On top of a Petoskey stone from the lake near George's home in Michigan, I rearrange shells from Scottish and Pacific beaches I walked with Jerry after George died. A Westie figurine stands under a cactus, next to a tobacco offering left by a Lakota friend. At first, I hid my gifts. Leaving presents for the dead seemed like a pagan custom my relatives and neighbors wouldn't appreciate. But on each visit, I found some object—once an orange, other times plants—I had not left on the grave. One day on a child's grave beside a wreath of plastic flowers, I noticed a new toy bulldozer and two stuffed bears. Even in the most typical of us some impulse to rebellion lives.

Just before Memorial Day for the first five years after George died, a hired caretaker mowed the cemetery grass and used a weed whacker to chop off growth inside each grave plot. Each year, he chopped the plants on the grave a half inch high, lopping buds from flowers nearly ready to bloom, leaving naked stems to bake under the summer sun. I pictured him as a young man wearing headphones, hearing and seeing nothing as he minced the plants I'd tended. I yelled at cemetery officials and wrote pleading letters. I threatened to dig George up and move him to a military cemetery, leaving a large, empty hole where he had been. One summer, I placed beside each plant heavy metal markers painted with Latin names, hoping to inform passersby about the native perennials—and to break the weed whacker. I hauled stones to surround the grave plots. Finally, after my father died, I erected signs that plead, "Please Do Not Mow Hasselstrom or Snell." The hacking stopped.

Finished with my caretaking, I often rest on George's tombstone to look at the world spread around the hilltop. The Black Hills stand to the west, while on the east lie the loamy creekside meadows where we grazed our cows in winter and cut hay in summer. Closer to the cemetery on the east, along both sides of the railroad tracks, is the town of Hermosa. The new gymnasium protrudes like a wart on the modest brick building where I started school when I was nine years old. The postcard-perfect, little white church where I married for the first time has been remodeled, its sparkling white boards replaced with dingy-looking tin siding.

The burial ground was an empty grassy hillside when the first settlers were interred here. A hundred years ago, stagecoaches pulled by fast horses traveled this road once or twice a week between the gold mines in Deadwood and the closest civilized town: Cheyenne, Wyoming. Now a steady stream of trucks and cars rushing back and forth on the four-lane highway creates a cyclone of sound and exhaust. Two new houses, the first in a planned development, stand precariously on a couple of flat spots carved in the hillside beside the cemetery gates. Next to them is the volunteer fire department's new garage, built and paid for with contributions made in honor of several local citizens upon their deaths—including my father.

In this community I went to school, voted, fought prairie fires with my neighbors. Working to be a good citizen, I taught their children, obeyed speed limits, and paid taxes. Nevertheless, I always felt as if I were not plugged into the same socket as everyone else.

By contrast, my excursions to the cemetery are like visiting with friends. Near George's plot, I nod and apologize again to the stone over the shriveled deaf woman who terrified me in grade school. My father told me sternly how she lost her hearing while she nursed half the town's children through a scarlet fever epidemic in the 1920s. Those she couldn't save lie near her. Not far away is the banker whose wife's money furnished the bank's original capital. He foreclosed on the parents of some of those children. From his diminished acreage, I can almost see the big house he built.

I smile and wave at the blithe ghost of my father's mother, Ida. By the time I met her, she was stout and ill, but my father's stories brought her to life. While her St. Bernard stood guard, she fed disgruntled workers marching on Washington. I always pause at the leaning white marker over my father's half brother, Archie, a man I never met, though I have held his insulin syringe and his army medals—my father kept them in an old trunk with family photographs. Now I can envision Archie sitting with George under the cedar tree by the Hasselstrom graves, talking over military life. When my mother visits the cemetery now, she sits in a folding chair at the foot of my father's grave, staring at the birth and death dates on his stone. Beside it, her stone bears her birth date and a blank space where the date of her death will be engraved.

My memories of the people and the country I have known form a narrative in the same way they shaped my life. Sometimes I can pinpoint the day and hour an event occurred, can be sure who said what. Other times I'm uncertain, and even while I struggle to be precise, I wonder if the details matter. The people and places I know will last only as long as my life. When I die, those stories will not be buried beneath the soil of this cemetery to decompose with my flesh. Like all stories, human and otherwise, they will begin to spiral up and down, earth to sky, coyote to owl, to grass and rain.

Soon after George died, when friends were beginning to say I spent too much time among the graves, someone told me about a woman I'll call Gail. She, too, spent considerable time there, looking down on the crossroads where her sixteen-year-old daughter died after pulling onto the highway in front of a speeding car. As a community service, Gail volunteered to improve the cemetery.

She decided first to map the graves, but her search of old records was confusing. Some pages noted a burial date but gave no location. Walking among the tombstones, she found sunken rectangles where no burial was indicated by the documents. Back and forth she moved between papers and the earth, walking along the rows, outlining her personal map of the dead with an embroidery of tracks.

Frustrated, she decided to imitate the dowsers—water witches— who find wells in our neighborhood by carrying a willow switch back and forth until it dips toward the earth, indicating that water lies below. When no one would see her, she experimented, walking back and forth in the moonlight clutching the forks of a stick. When it dipped, she marked the spot on her map.

As she probed among old-timers' memories and searched the annals, she confirmed that in every case, someone was buried where the rod dipped.

How could a woman with a twig locate abandoned graves? A normal adult body is sixty to seventy percent water, the substance most necessary for human survival next to air. Maybe water, and blood, continue to whisper underground long after their host body has decomposed.

On one fall trip to the cemetery, I saw Gail working at her daughter's grave. I pulled weeds slowly, hoping she'd speak, thinking that we might enjoy talking with one another—two women obsessed with death.

First she shoveled the pink quartz over the grave into buckets. Then she tore away the black plastic under it. Finally, she lifted from the trunk of her car a half dozen immense prickly pear cactus and put them in shallow holes.

Finished, she nodded and came to stand beside me. "I like your native plants," she said, "so I decided to do the same."

"Did you know they outlawed cacti at the same time they banned trees? Said when someone mows the cactus plants, every little shred sprouts into a new cactus."

"Yep," she said, grinning. "That's why. Nobody's going to mow them off. And the caretaker kept moving the things I left for my daughter, like her yearbook. No more!"

I nodded at her. "That daylily on George's grave has been here five years, and I haven't seen it bloom yet."

We grinned at each other, cunning protectors of our dead. Sitting at the foot of George's grave, we compared notes. Like two adolescents sharing secrets, we discovered we both come to the cemetery at odd hours.

"You nearly tripped over me one night," she said. "When I saw your car lights, I hid behind that lilac bush. Thought you were a carload of teenage drunks." I told her of spending one Fourth of July crouched behind the cemetery cannons, watching the town fireworks and trying not to be seen by the kids having a beer party on the other side of the lilac bushes. "For some reason, that makes me think of Whitman's line," I told her. "'The beautiful uncut hair of graves.'"

She nodded. "And Sandburg: 'I am the grass. Let me work.'"

Acknowledgments

I thank the many people who helped me during the eight years I worked on this book, including (but not limited to):

Jerry, for steadfast encouragement and calm, if no plumbing is required;

Bryan Jones, who sacrificed his own writing time to comment on drafts of these essays over and over, month after month and year after year, proving once more that a good critic, like a bull elk in September, sometimes has to be meaner than dirt;

Gina, Liz, and all who knew Vallecitos Retreat, including Emilia, who built the adobe house and whose spirit encouraged me as I worked on these essays in the loft room;

Cathy, Lorraine, Nancy, Suzan, and Mindy, for their unfailing friendship and honesty as well as their suggestions.

Thanks also to the clerk in the Custer County, South Dakota, Treasurer's Office, who symbolizes the difference between a neighborhood and just a place to live. My first check for property taxes on my ranch was ten cents short. She added the dime from her pocket.

And to H. C. Berger's Red Banshee, a delicious local beer, for warming me clear to my toes on long dark nights.

Early versions of some essays were previously published as follows:

"Blues for Shoveling Horse Manure" was published by *High Plains Register,* Laramie County Community College, Spring 1998, pp. 53–57.

"Reckoning the Cost of a Dead Steer" was published as fiction ("The Price of Bullets") in *Missouri Review,* vol. 22, no. 1, 1989, pp. 7–16.

"Looking for the Dark: Buffalo Winter" was published in *American Literary Review,* Fall 1994, guest editor W. Scott Olsen, pp. 39–48. In *The Best American Essays of 1995,* Jamaica Kincaid and Robert Atwan cited "Buffalo Winter" as one of the "Notable Essays" of 1994.

"Badger's Business" was published in *weber studies,* guest editor Louis Owens, editor Sherwin W. Howard, Winter 1999, vol. 16, no. 2, pp. 94–103; and in a parallel electronic edition of the journal via the World Wide Web.

"Lightning Strikes the White Heifer" was published (as "Looking for Life: Lightning") in *North Dakota Quarterly,* Fall 1996, pp. 20–25.

"Nighthawks Fly in Thunderstorms" was published (as "Flying in Thunderstorms") in *The Soul of Nature: Visions of a Living Earth,* Michael Tobias and Georgianne Cowan, editors (New York: Continuum, 1994), pp. 65–74.

Parts of other essays were published in different arrangements and under different titles, as follows:

"Finding My Way," part of the prologue, was published by *High Country News,* November 16, 1995.

"City Home," part of the prologue, was published in *Where the Heart Is,* Julienne Bennett and Mimi Luebbermann, editors, Wildcat Canyon Press, 1995, p. 24, with a brief excerpt in the same book, p. 20.

"Going Back to Grass," part of "The Young Cow," was published in *North Dakota Quarterly,* Winter 1997, vol. 64, no. 1, pp. 5–14.

"Opening the Gates," including parts of several other essays, and "The Bulls: Symphony of Discord," including part of "Climbing into the Bull Pen," were published in *North Dakota Quarterly,* Winter 1997, vol. 64, no. 4, pp. 5–20.

———————

Note to perceptive readers who noticed I gave thanks for beer: These days, when more and more people buy advice on conducting their lives neatly packaged as *10 Rules for a Perfect Whatever,* I feel compelled to explain that I'm not suggesting that buying or consuming liquor will make you a better writer. Quite the contrary. Don't expect anyone else to make rules you can live by. Shut out the honking horns, the insistent voices. Find a way to go on, on your own terms.

© Jerry L. Ellerman

Linda Hasselstrom is the award-winning author of three previous books of poetry, including *Windbreak,* and several nonfiction books. She is a coeditor of *Leaning into the Wind* and, most recently, *Woven on the Wind.* Hasselstrom's work has appeared in numerous publications and has been featured in *The Best American Essays 1995, The Best American Essays 1997,* and *American Nature Writing.* She divides her time between her ranch in Wyoming and her home in South Dakota.